GOD IS IN THE SMALL STUFF

BRUCE & STAN

GOD IS IN THE SMALL STUFF

BRUCE & STAN

Gift Edition

© 1998 by Bruce Bickel and Stan Jantz

ISBN 978-1-62029-162-7

All rights reserved. No part of this publication may be reproduced or transmitted for commercial purposes, except for brief quotations in printed reviews, without written permission of the publisher.

Churches and other noncommercial interests may reproduce portions of this book without the express written permission of Barbour Publishing, provided that the text does not exceed 500 words and that the text is not material quoted from another publisher. When reproducing text from this book, include the following credit line: "From God Is in the Small Stuff by Bruce Bickel and Stan Jantz, published by Barbour Publishing, Inc. Used by permission."

Scripture quotations marked NLT are taken from the *Holy Bible*, New Living Translation, copyright 1996. Used by permission of Tyndale House Publishers, Inc., Wheaton, Illinois 60189, USA. All rights reserved.

Scripture marked NIV is from the HOLY BIBLE: NEW INTERNATIONAL VERSION®. NIV®. Copyright © 1973, 1978, 1984 by Biblica, Inc.™ Used by permission. All rights reserved worldwide.

Published by Barbour Publishing, Inc., P.O. Box 719, Uhrichsville, Ohio 44683, www.barbourbooks.com

Our mission is to publish and distribute inspirational products offering exceptional value and biblical encouragement to the masses.

Member of the
Evangelical Christian
Publishers Association

Printed in China.

Contents

Introduction 7
1. Understand the Nature of God 11
2. Get to Know God Better 17
3. Realize That God Loves You 23
4. You Can Know God's Will 29
5. God Wants You to Grow 35
6. The Bible: God's Message to You 41
7. Give God Time 47
8. Prayer: The Great Connector 53
9. Church: Where God's People Gather 59
10. Appreciate God's Creation 65
11. Character: What Happens When
    No One's Looking 71
12. What Would Jesus Do? 77
13. Discipline Yourself (No One Else Will) 83
14. Improve Yourself (No One Else Can) 89
15. Your Body Is a Temple 95
16. Simplify Life and Enjoy It More 101
17. Arrange Your Priorities 107
18. Contentment Is Good for the Soul 113
19. Stop Worrying and Start Living 119

20.	Embrace Adversity	125
21.	The God Who Comforts Us	131
22.	Learn to Read	137
23.	Learn to Write	143
24.	Communication Is More Than Talking	149
25.	Encouragement Is a Gift	155
26.	Leadership Is an Art	161
27.	Money: Learn to Deal with It	167
28.	A Generous Spirit Works Wonders	173
29.	Compassion: Much More Than Pity	179
30.	Laugh and the World Laughs With You	185
31.	Criticize and You Walk Alone	191
32.	Relationships Take Time	197
33.	How to Really Love Your Spouse	203
34.	The Perfect Gift for Your Young Child	209
35.	How to Really Love Your Teenager	215
36.	When Your Child Leaves Home	221
37.	Families Are Forever	227
38.	You Need Your Friends	233
39.	Carpe Diem: Seize the Day	239
40.	God Is in the Small Stuff	245
	About the Authors	251

Introduction

A popular book suggests that you don't worry about the small stuff. We agree, but we take exception to any idea that the small stuff isn't important. In fact, we want to encourage you to closely examine and cherish the seemingly everyday, ordinary circumstances of your life. Why? Because God is in the details of your life.

Imagine that! The almighty Creator of the universe is interested and active in the details of your life. He cares about what you are doing and thinking. He wants to comfort you in times of despair, pressure, and problems. He wants to uplift your spirit and guide you through life's tough decisions. He wants to weave the everyday "threads" of your life into a divinely designed "tapestry."

Sometimes it's easy to sense God's presence when you observe His handiwork in nature. You see His majesty in the snow-covered mountains; you feel His serenity in a starry night. These are dramatic reminders of the enormity of God, but contemplating God in nature often leaves us with a lopsided understanding of Him. We think about God as vast, immense, and impersonal.

The purpose of this book is to help you see God at His personal best. God created the universe, but He also created you. God knows *you*, God loves *you*, and God cares about the smallest details of *your* life.

> *So I tell you, don't worry about everyday life—*
> *whether you have enough food, drink, and clothes.*
> *Doesn't life consist of more than food and clothing?*
> *Look at the birds. They don't need to plant or harvest*
> *or put food in barns because your heavenly Father*
> *feeds them. And you are far more valuable to him*
> *than they are.*
>
> MATTHEW 6:25–26 NLT

We are convinced that you will learn much more about God (and yourself) as you begin to recognize God's involvement in the everyday details of life. "What makes God so clear to us," wrote Oswald Chambers, "is not so much His big blessings to us, but the tiny things, because they show His amazing intimacy with us—He knows every detail of each of our individual lives."

This book contains forty short essays to guide you on your journey to discover God in the details. At the end of each essay, we've included a list of contemporary "proverbs" and suggestions to focus your thoughts on the "small stuff" in your life.

We hope and pray that you will be overwhelmed by God's love as you begin to see Him in the small stuff of your life. . .that you will begin to recognize His plan in the details and seemingly ordinary circumstances. . .and that you will connect with God in a more meaningful way as you choose to follow His personally designed plan for you.

Bruce & Stan

Do you not know?
Have you not heard?
The LORD is the everlasting God,
the Creator of the ends of the earth.
He will not grow tired or weary,
and his understanding
no one can fathom.

Isaiah 40:28 NIV

ONE

Understand the Nature of God

Who is God? Is He a mystery to you? Do you want to know Him better? Maybe you wonder if God even exists. That's okay. People have wondered about God for as long as...well, for as long as there have been people. They wonder if He's really out there. They wonder if He made the world and everything in it. And if He did, they wonder if God still cares about what's going on.

Perhaps you've gotten past all of those questions. You

definitely believe in God, but you don't know Him. You don't understand His nature—in other words, His personality. You aren't alone. For many people—even those who claim to be religious—the nature of God is a mystery. It's like God is behind some dark cloud, occasionally speaking in a deep voice to prophets and such (you know, like He spoke to Charleton Heston in *The Ten Commandments*). Other people think God wants to prevent them from having a good time. If they get close to God, they're afraid they'll have to give up their freedom.

While it's true there are things about God we'll never know (after all, He is God), there are many things we *can* know. For example, when we look at our universe—whether it's through a microscope, a telescope, or the naked eye—we observe incredible design and order and beauty. That means the Designer (that would be God) must be a being of design and order and beauty. And He must be pretty powerful.

When we look at ourselves and see that we all have some idea about God (even when you deny God exists, you have to think about Him), that means the Creator (God again) put that idea in us. Yet God is more than an idea. He is more than a symbol for good or an impersonal "higher being." God is a very real spirit Being who has always existed in the past, who exists now, and will always exist in the future. God is personal. God is involved in our world. And God has revealed His nature to us. All we have to do is stop, look, and listen.

...In the Small Stuff

- God knows what's in our hearts. We might as well get right to the point.

- Remember that God values you for who you are, not what you do.

- True faith involves doing all you can and letting God take care of the rest.

- God will never send a thirsty soul to a dry well.
- God speaks. Do you listen?
- God commands. Do you obey?
- God leads. Do you follow?
- God is more likely to speak to you with a gentle whisper than with a loud voice.
- God won't take away a sin until you give it over to Him.
- The times when you need God the most are when you don't think you need Him.
- Faith is not an emotion. It is objective trust placed in a very real God.
- The way you think about God does not define Him.

- One quality of God's nature that should make us tremble is His justice.

- One quality of God's nature that should give us comfort is His love.

- Don't worry about proving God's existence, because no one can disprove it.

- You can't network, strong-arm, or sweet-talk your way into heaven. Your faith is all that counts.

- Religion is man's attempt to find God. The Gospel is God's plan to reach man. Don't let religion stand in the way of your salvation.

- Thank God that your salvation does not depend on you.

Then the way you live will always honor and please the Lord... All the while, you will learn to know God better and better.

Colossians 1:10 NLT

TWO

GET TO KNOW
GOD BETTER

Does God seem distant? Is He detached from you? Maybe that's because you are waiting for God to come to you. If so, then you've got things backwards.

God has given us His Word, His Son, and His Spirit. That is more than we will ever need in order to understand God (and certainly more than we can absorb in a lifetime). But the next step belongs to each of us. It's up to us to read

God's Word, to believe in His Son, and to follow the guidance of the Holy Spirit.

You see, God is a perfect gentleman. He never forces Himself on anyone. He anxiously desires a deep and meaningful personal relationship with you, but He won't force the issue. It must be voluntary on your part. So, if you want to get to know God better, *you* must approach *Him*. When Jesus taught about this principle, He presented the relationship as an invitation:

> *Look! Here I stand at the door and knock. If you hear me calling and open the door, I will come in, and we will share a meal as friends.*
> REVELATION 3:20 NLT

God makes Himself available, but you must respond to His invitation. Take Him at His Word. Go to Him. Open the door of your heart to Him.

You don't have to move to a monastery to know God

better. You don't have to learn ancient Hebrew or memorize the names of the twelve disciples in alphabetical order. All it takes is your time and attention—reading His Word and talking to Him. Start with a few minutes each day, and grow from there. You don't have to call to schedule an appointment. He has already extended the invitation, and He's waiting for you to respond.

...In the Small Stuff

- There is a direct relationship between the desire to know God and the struggle that follows.

- Never be ashamed of your faith.

- Feeling good about God does not bring you closer to Him.

- God's anger lasts only for a moment, but His favor lasts a lifetime.

- You are responsible for the depth of your spiritual understanding. God is responsible for the breadth of your ministry.

- Seek to know God and faith will follow.

- To love God is to obey God.

- Rather than worry about what you don't know about God, concentrate on what you know.

- Love God, not godliness.

- Discover what pleases God, and then make them habits.

- Exposing yourself to God's truth is risky, but it's a risk worth taking.

- The highest learning is to know God and, from that knowledge, to love Him.

- Knowing God takes tremendous effort, but the reward is great.

- Get a concordance and look up the names of God.

- Get a concordance and study the names of Jesus.

- You begin to seek God for who He is when you stop seeking Him for what He can do for you.

- Ask the Lord to teach you His ways.

- Have a passion for God and compassion for people.

This is real love.
It is not that we loved God,
but that he loved us...

1 John 4:10 NLT

THREE

Realize That God Loves You

Love is a powerful emotion, perhaps the strongest of human emotions. People will go to great lengths to express love, and they will do almost anything to get love. So if love is in such demand, why does it seem in such short supply? To paraphrase the song, "Why is love the only thing that there's just too little of?"

The problem with human love is that it's usually self-centered. Much of the so-called love we feel could be summarized by the phrase, "What's in it for me?" We may think we love someone, but in reality we may simply love what he or she does for us.

The great writer C. S. Lewis identified four different kinds of love, all but one of which are basically self-centered. First, there's *affection*, which is the kind of love we can have for something other than people, such as a dog or a home or a car. Then there's *friendship*, a valuable love in the sense that it's the basis of most human relationships. And there's *erotic* love, which is beautiful between a husband and wife but a mess outside of married love. All of these are wonderful and necessary loves, but each of them depends on the object of our affection for complete fulfillment.

The only love that is completely other-centered is called *agape* love. This is love of the highest order. It's what Lewis called "Divine Gift-Love." When we love with *agape* love we desire the best for the people we love. We are even able to love those who are unlovable.

We are capable of *agape* love only to the extent that we give the details of our lives over to God and allow Him to work in us. But even before that can happen, we must realize that God loves us, and that He can only love us with this kind of love. God's love is never self-centered, and God's love is always sacrificial. While we were enemies of God, He loved us. When we ran from God, He loved us. And He loved us so much that He sacrificed the Son He loved most so that we could experience eternal life.

Love is the essence of God. Love is what motivates Him to do what He does for us—down to the last detail—even when we don't love Him in return. Knowing that should give tremendous meaning to our lives.

...In the Small Stuff

- Whenever you feel insignificant, remember how important you are to God.

- We love God because we know who He is. God loves us despite who we are.

- Love yourself as the unique individual God created you to be—nothing more, nothing less.

- Unconditional love comes only from our Heavenly Father.

- God does not help us because we deserve it; He helps us because He loves us.

- Find your self-worth in God's unconditional love for you, not your accomplishments.

- The love of God has no limits.

- The reason we can love God is because He loved us first.

- God's unconditional love for us should motivate us to love others unconditionally.

- Never confuse love with lust.

- Love isn't an option. We are commanded by God to love others.

- Loving God is the greatest thing you can do.

If you believe,
you will receive whatever
you ask for in prayer.

Matthew 21:22 NLT

FOUR

You Can Know God's Will

God's will is a paradox. It's both easy to find and difficult to discern. God's will can be immediate, or it may take years to figure out. God's will can frustrate you or give you tremendous peace.

One thing is for sure. You *can* know God's will. Although it may seem mysterious, there's really no mystery to it. If you know where to look, God's will is there. And if you listen carefully, God will speak to you in amazing ways.

First of all, God speaks through His Word, the Bible. Everything we need for living a life that pleases God—and what could be more in His will than that—is in the Bible. As you get to know God's Word, you will get to know God's will.

Second, God speaks through your own judgment and common sense. But beware. Your decisions will line up with God's will only if you know God personally in the first place, and then only if your relationship with God is right. When you're in this condition, you will operate with "the mind of Christ." The Holy Spirit will guide you from the inside.

Finally, and most commonly, God speaks through the details of your life. Oswald Chambers put it this way: "God speaks in the language you know best—not through your ears but through your circumstances."

You think your life is an accident? Not a chance. You're here for a reason. And what you do matters to God. Everything. Not just the stuff you do in church or Bible study (although that is very important), but in the everyday small stuff. That's where you'll find God's will most often.

Take a look at your life. Think about the moments and events—the details—and see how far you've come. Those "good things" weren't coincidences. You weren't just "lucky." If your heart has followed after God, then God has been leading you, and you have been doing His will, perhaps without even knowing it.

On the other hand, if you feel like life is dealing you one bad hand after another, and you feel sorry for yourself—and you're mad at God—maybe it's time to get back to basics. Take the focus off yourself and get to know God better by reading His Word, praying, and associating with people who are in God's will. God wants to direct you through the details of your life. Give Him a chance.

...In the Small Stuff

- God's plans are always perfect. That said, seek His will.

- Don't make plans and then ask for the Lord's approval. Ask God to direct your planning.

- If you're going to wait for someone, wait for the Lord.

- God may be using people who disagree with you.

- The call of God is sometimes difficult to hear.

- Once discerned, the call of God is difficult to avoid.

- Remember that God's will is not so much a function of time and place as it is an attitude of the heart.

- If you want to know God's will, spend time with Him.

- No one can please God without adding a great deal of happiness to his or her own life.

- Circumstances may be outside your control, but the way you respond to them is not.

- When you feel like settling for less than the best, think about what God wants for you.

- You will begin to live when you lose yourself in God's purpose for you.

- When God speaks, listen.

- When God commands, obey.

- When God leads, follow.

Dear brothers and sisters...
we are thankful that
your faith is flourishing
and you are all growing
in love for each other.

2 Thessalonians 1:3 NLT

FIVE

God Wants You to Grow

When it comes to progress, there are no shortcuts. If you want to improve in any area of your life, you have to pay attention to the small stuff. You have to take one step at a time.

Say you want to get into shape physically or lose some weight (or both). Contrary to the promises made by miracle programs, machines, and drugs, there is no such thing as instant success. You have to pay attention to the details by eating and exercising correctly every day in order to realize long-term results. The same principle applies to improving your mind. There's no quick way to get a college degree. And even if a diploma isn't your goal, the only way to accumulate useful knowledge is through disciplined, consistent study. You can't even train a dog overnight! It takes repetition, consistency, reinforcement, and practice. Otherwise your canine companion will look at you as if to say, "You've got to be kidding!"

Well, we're not kidding. It's a fact of life. To grow in any area, you've got to do the little things over and over again. The principle of growth through detail is especially true in your spiritual life, yet people think that by praying once in a while (when they get in trouble), by going to church twice a year (on Christmas and Easter, of course), and by cracking open a Bible once in a blue moon, God will smile on them and give them blessing upon blessing.

Make no mistake about it. God won't love you any more just because you do certain things. His love for you is always the highest love. But you will experience certain spiritual benefits if you pay attention to spiritual details. Like reading the Bible consistently. Or talking to God on a regular basis. Or helping others in need when the need is clear. We're not talking about spiritual legalism. Paying attention to the details of your spiritual life is all about *discipline*.

God wants you to grow spiritually because when you do, your life becomes more meaningful and more satisfying. Just like you feel when you make the consistent effort to improve physically, you will feel great about yourself when you make the effort to improve spiritually. And even better than that, the people around you will experience the benefits of your growth.

...In the Small Stuff

- Recognize that you can't get holy in a hurry.
- Little is much if God is in it.

- A spiritually mature individual places more importance on God's internal presence than on the world's external signs.

- The person who looks up to God rarely looks down on anyone.

- It's better to run behind God than in front of Him.

- Rejoice in the Lord's discipline as well as His blessings.

- Live the Christian life as if the Lord were guiding your steps.

- Be cautious in telling others what you can do, but be bold in asserting what God can do.

- The person dependent on Christ has the amazing ability to maintain a steady ship on a stormy sea.

- Realize your inadequacy without God and your sufficiency with God.

- Faith does not demand miracles, but often accomplishes them.

- Make God's provision the foundation of your performance.

- You will never be humble before God if you think He needs you.

- It's a good thing to delight in the Lord, but how much better when the Lord delights in you.

Your word is
a lamp for my feet
and a light
for my path.

Psalm 119:105 NLT

SIX

THE BIBLE: GOD'S MESSAGE TO YOU

The Bible is the world's most amazing book. More than six billion copies of the Bible have been published since Gutenberg printed the first one five hundred years ago. The Bible has been translated into more than two thousand languages (and counting). More than ninety percent of all households in America have at least one Bible, and nearly four out of every ten people claim to read the Bible at least once a week, not counting church. No other book has even come close to the Bible's popularity and influence.

The Bible is the world's all-time best-seller for one very simple reason: It's God's book. You may not think of God as an author, but that's exactly what He is. God is the author, and *you* are the audience He wants to reach. You see, authors want people to read their books (otherwise they wouldn't write them). God is no different. He's written the Bible, and He wants you to read it.

So why a book? Why not voice commands or mental telepathy or skywriting? Because human language—especially when it's written down—is the most effective and accurate way to communicate. God chose to speak to us through words on a page because it's the best way to communicate the details of His message to us.

What does this mean to you? Simply this. When you read the Bible, you are reading God's message for you. The Bible is not just an option for knowing God and the secrets of the universe. It's the *only* way for you to accurately discover the details of God's plan for you. For example, through the

Bible you can learn that God created you. You can discover that God loved you so much that He sent Jesus to earth so you could see what God is like in person. And you can find out that Jesus is coming back to earth again in the future.

The Bible has all of that and more. So don't waste another day. Dust off that Bible in your house and open it. As you read, God will begin to speak to you. And what He has to say may very well change your life.

...In the Small Stuff

- If you don't have a Bible, get one.

- If you've got a Bible, read it.

- If you read the Bible, believe it.

- If you believe the Bible, live it.

- Appreciate the commands of Scripture as much as the promises.

- Keep a Bible by your bed.

- Live what the Bible teaches. Don't merely quote the Scripture.

- A Bible on the shelf is worthless; a Bible being read is priceless.

- Keep a notepad in your Bible.

- Stand up when you hear the Word of God.

- Studying the Bible is like feeding your soul spiritual food.

- Make a daily habit to read the chapter in Proverbs that corresponds to the current date.

- Read one of Paul's epistles each week and feel inspired. When you finish, start over.

- Learn to appreciate poetry—read the Psalms.

- If you're wondering how God speaks, commands, and leads—read the Bible.

- The next time you take your Bible for granted, remember that in some countries it's illegal to own a Bible.

- If you think of the Bible as God's personal letter to you, you might end up reading it as often as you read your mail.

- God's Word is eternal.

- The Bible is a gift meant to be shared with others.

Be still in
the presence of the Lord,
and wait patiently
for him to act.

Psalm 37:7 NLT

SEVEN

Give God Time

If there's one thing we need in the midst of our busy, loud, and nervous lives, it's the inner peace and quiet and assurance that only God can give. It's the only way to see God's purposes for us, let alone keep our sanity.

The thing is, God doesn't yell out and say, "Hey, you're neglecting me. Sit still for a moment so you can hear me." Oh, He is fully capable of getting our attention when we really need it, but you don't want to make a habit of giving God a reason to chase you down (and He will).

Rather than waiting for God to whack you over the head with a spiritual two-by-four, wouldn't it be far better to give God some time each day to quietly speak to you? Actually, this is God's preference. "Be silent, and know that I am God!" He says (Psalm 46:10 NLT). Being still may be the hardest thing you will ever do, but it may be the most important. Look at it this way. When you give God time, you show Him respect. In effect you're saying, "God, You're important enough to me to set aside some time each day. I want You to teach me, and I want to learn."

Will God talk to you if you let Him? Most definitely. Not in an audible voice, but through your thoughts and emotions. God also talks through His Word, the Bible. Remember, the Bible is God's voice for us. The only way to hear it is to read it.

The doorway to letting God into the details of your life—into your concerns and dreams—is time. We know this won't be easy. Many other voices will call out for your time and attention, and many of them are worthwhile. But if you want to hear the one Voice who will make all the difference in your life, you'll need to let God in. . .quietly.

Ask God to give you the desire to set aside a place and a time just for Him. The details of your life will wait. More than that, they'll take on more meaning when you give them over to God.

. . .In the Small Stuff

- Make an appointment with God every day and then keep it as if you were meeting with the most important person in the world.

- Set aside a designated period of time each day, each week, each month, and each year to focus on God.

- The advantage of meeting God at the same time each day is that you don't have to decide when you are going to do it.

- Sometime in the next month, try giving the Lord a day out of your life. An entire day.

- Make moments of stillness, quiet, and solitude part of your daily routine.

- Rising early to meet the Lord gives you a jump on the day. Meeting God at night enables you to reflect on the day. Either option is good.

- If you hurry through life without giving God time, this world will seem like a hospital, a place to get sick and die.

- If you go through life with God, this world will seem like an inn, a place to stay while you're passing through.

- Buy a book of blank pages and keep a journal. Even if you only write a few words. Record your spiritual and personal thoughts and feelings as you give God time each day.

- Time cannot be controlled. You can only control yourself.

- Depending on your spiritual condition, being alone with God will either be unnerving or invigorating.

- The time to find moments of stillness and quiet is when it's the most difficult to do so.

The eyes of the Lord
watch over those who do right,
and his ears are open
to their prayers.

1 Peter 3:12 NLT

EIGHT

Prayer: The Great Connector

One day the disciples requested of Jesus: "Teach us to pray." Jesus responded by giving them—and us—a marvelous model of prayer. What is so powerful about the Lord's Prayer, as it is known, is its utter simplicity.

> *Our Father in heaven, may your name be honored. May your kingdom come soon. May your*

> *will be done here on earth, just as it is in heaven. Give us our food for today, and forgive us our sins, just as we have forgiven those who have sinned against us. And don't let us yield to temptation, but deliver us from the evil one.*
>
> MATTHEW 6:9–13 NLT

The key to prayer is to start simply and quietly. That's the idea behind Jesus' model prayer. We need a touchstone, a place to start. Then, as we get to know God better, we will feel comfortable sharing the most intimate details of our lives with Him.

If the Bible is God talking to us, then prayer is us talking to God. It's the primary way of connecting to the infinite, all-powerful, all-knowing, all-loving God. Edward Ferrell wrote that "without prayer, there is no way, no truth, no life." Without prayer, you can never get close to God.

Try it. Start small. Start with the small stuff in your life. Talk to God about it in a quiet, isolated place where your self-consciousness isn't an issue. As you continue daily, your capacity for prayer will grow larger. That's because prayer is like a muscle. If you exercise it regularly, your prayer muscle will gain strength and your appreciation for God will grow immeasurably. On the other hand, if you don't use it, your prayer muscle will shrivel up and your capacity for God will shrink. And in those times of crisis when you suddenly feel compelled to pray, it will likely be a painful experience.

The good news is that God doesn't put conditions on your prayer life. His feelings don't get hurt when you don't pray. But when you do, He connects with you in a powerful way. Try it today. Try it right now. Talk to God. He's listening.

...IN THE SMALL STUFF

- Prayer changes things.
- Pray for people who dislike you.

- Pray for people you dislike.

- When you pray, be careful to distinguish your needs from your desires.

- Prayer without effort will be insincere. Effort without prayer will be ineffective.

- If your prayers don't mean anything to you, they mean even less to God.

- Live humbly and pray likewise.

- Don't pray for a lighter load. Pray for a stronger back.

- Become quiet before God in the busiest and noisiest part of your day.

- Prayer involves listening to God as well as speaking to Him.

- You can't stand up to Satan if you don't kneel before God.

- Pray with perseverance and expectancy.

- At its core, prayer is giving yourself to God.

- Pray as if the task depends on God and work as if it depends on you.

- The next time you feel weak in the knees, try using them to pray.

- There is no such thing as a successful or unsuccessful prayer.

- People of God may not talk about their prayer habits, but their lives speak volumes.

And let us not neglect
our meeting together,
as some people do...

Hebrews 10:25 NLT

NINE

CHURCH: WHERE GOD'S PEOPLE GATHER

Ever so innocently, we've let our English language distort the meaning of the word *church*. Sometimes, that word means a *place* (as in "I left my Bible at church"). Other times, it refers to an *activity* (as in "What time does *church* start?"). Often *church* is used to describe an *institution* (as in "His behavior was frowned upon by the *church*"). While such definitions are appropriate, they miss the meaning of what *church* is all about.

The essence of *church* is your Christian family—those people around the world who follow Christ and commit themselves to Him and to each other. When the apostle Paul wrote about the church, he wasn't talking about a building, an activity, or an institution. For Paul, the expression of *church* meant a personal relationship among Christians. He most often compared the *church* to a human body.

In a body, all the parts and details are important, and they must function in harmony:

- If one member of the body is injured or sick, then the entire body suffers.
- The members must operate in unison, because if they try to go in opposite directions, they won't get anywhere.
- Some members are more visible, while others play a vital role on the inside. But both types are necessary. There are no small parts in the body of Christ.

- If every member were the same, the body would look really weird, and it wouldn't function very well. (Just imagine a five-foot, eight-inch ear. Oh sure, you would have excellent hearing, but try driving a car that way.)

The next time you go to church, don't look at the building or think about the schedule of events. Instead, look at the people. Appreciate them for who they are, what they need, and what they contribute to the "body." Then think about yourself. What is your role in the church? How do you fit into the body? Are you making a contribution to the overall health and fitness of the body?

Being part of the church means a lot more than just attending a service on Sunday morning, tossing a few coins in the basket, and shaking the pastor's hand on the way out. Being a part of the church involves an interactive relationship between people with Christ as their common bond. With that definition, you can't "walk out of the church" on Sunday morning. You are part of the body all week long.

...In the Small Stuff

- Get involved at church.

- Here's how to make Sunday worship more meaningful: Think of yourself as a participant rather than a spectator.

- If God hasn't called you to be a church leader, be careful how you criticize those who are.

- Express appreciation to your pastor.

- Don't leave the sermon at church.

- Give money to your church regularly.

- Teach a Sunday School class at least once a year.

- Next time you're in church, sit in the front row. You'll be amazed how much more you'll learn (not to mention how it will affect the pastor).

- If you tend to fall asleep in church, sit in the back row. You can lean your head against the wall so it doesn't snap forward when you doze off.

- The measure of a good sermon is the listener's response, not the pastor's speech.

- It is true that Christianity is good. More important, Christianity is true.

The heavens tell
of the glory of God.
The skies display
his marvelous
craftsmanship.

Psalm 19:1 NLT

TEN

APPRECIATE GOD'S CREATION

The world in which we live is one of the greatest proofs for the existence of God. The very fact that the universe exists at all points to a Creator. Even the most cynical scientist does not believe that everything around us came from nothing. There had to be a beginning. And if there was a beginning, there had to be Someone to begin everything (Genesis 1:1).

But God didn't just create the world; He *designed* it. Whether you study the cosmos or the human body, you will find that the systems and cycles and rhythms of life operate with incredible precision. And like many others, including a large number of the world's top scientists, you will conclude that all of it came from an intelligent Designer, who is powerful, personal, and loving.

The apostle Paul put it this way:

> *From the time the world was created, people have seen the earth and sky and all that God made. They can clearly see his invisible qualities—his eternal power and divine nature. So they have no excuse whatsoever for not knowing God.*
> ROMANS 1:20 NLT

Yet in spite of the evidence around us, people have done a strange thing. They have chosen to focus on the creation rather than the Creator. Paul wrote that people worship "the things God made but not the Creator himself" (Romans 1:25 NLT). That would be like seeing a beautiful painting and concluding that the artist had nothing to do with it, or that the artist really didn't matter. We just don't do that. We acknowledge and praise the artist while showing appreciation for the painting.

The same thing goes for God's creation. We are to appreciate it, protect it, and even manage it while preserving it. But we should never worship creation. All praise should go to the Creator, God Almighty.

...In the Small Stuff

- Your view of the world and how it works is directly related to your view of origins.

- Your view of origins will determine your worldview.

- When it comes to origins, there are only two alternatives: Either God created the heavens and the earth, or He didn't.

- If God didn't create the heavens and the earth, they happened by themselves.

- It is impossible for something to come from nothing.

- Don't get hung up on *how long ago* God made the heavens and the earth.

- Don't get hung up on *how long it took* God to make the heavens and the earth.

- If you want to know yourself better, get to know your Creator better.

- It is our responsibility to use and manage—not abuse and deplete—our natural resources.

- When you see a beautiful painting, praise the artist.

- When you hear a beautiful song, praise the composer.

- When you experience beauty in nature, praise the Creator.

- Take time to appreciate God's created world.

- Science is not the enemy of God, and religion is not the enemy of science. After all, when God made the world, He made science possible.

- You can learn a great deal about God by studying His creation.

May integrity and
honesty protect me,
for I put my hope
in you.

Psalm 25:21 NLT

ELEVEN

CHARACTER: WHAT HAPPENS WHEN NO ONE'S LOOKING

One of the great debates of the last few years has centered on character. Some people believe that it's possible for a person to possess both a public and a private character, even if the two are very different. What you do in private, the reasoning goes, is your own business, as long as it doesn't affect your public performance.

There's only one problem with this thinking. Once

you divide your personality and your actions into two or more categories or compartments, you deviate from the very definition of character. At its root, *character* is defined by *integrity*, and at the heart of integrity is the idea of *wholeness*. If an object (such as a bridge) or a person (such as you) has integrity, it means that the object or person is in an unbroken condition. Therefore, if your character—which defines who you are—is broken into two or more pieces, you no longer have integrity. And without integrity, you don't have much character.

Recall the story of the *Titanic* (either the real event or the movie version). One of the primary reasons the big boat was considered unsinkable was because of the compartments in its hull. The theory was that flooding in one compartment due to a breach (that's a broken place) in the hull wouldn't affect other compartments because of the high walls between them. What the *Titanic's* designers did not anticipate was that the collision with the iceberg slashed through several compartments at once, so that the sea water spilled over the walls from one compartment to another until the mighty ship tragically sank.

The same thing applies to life. You think you can keep a break in one part of your life from impacting the other parts, but it just doesn't work that way. An integrity breach in one compartment of your life quickly spills over to another until your entire life begins to sink.

So how do you keep your life from flooding? It all has to do with integrity. Keeping your life together. Living your life in private the way you do in public, and vice versa. When you live your life as a whole rather than in parts, you can handle breaks (and you will have them) because there are caring people around who will help you repair the damage—if they know about it.

One of the best ways to keep your life whole is to pay attention to the small stuff. Do what it takes every day to develop your character and preserve your integrity. Most of all don't live your life to please others. Live your life to please God.

...In the Small Stuff

- The manner in which you cultivate your inner garden will be evident to all manner of pests.

- People of integrity make an easy target for critics because they stand upright.

- Let your word be your bond: Keep your promises, meet your deadlines, honor your commitments, pay your bills.

- It's one thing to know what's right, and another thing entirely to do it.

- Others determine your reputation. You determine your character.

- If you want to know what's in your heart, listen to your mouth.

- If you find yourself in a questionable situation, get out immediately.

- Before you can ask integrity of others, you must attempt to be blameless yourself.

- The practice of honesty is more convincing than the profession of holiness.

- Character is made by what you stand for; reputation by what you fall for.

- Take a little more than your share of the blame.

- Take a little less than your share of the credit.

- Be honest with yourself. Be honest with other people. Be honest with God.

- Character is one of those qualities that takes time to develop.

- Rest on God's promises; stand behind yours.

Those who say
they live in God
should live their lives
as Christ did.

1 John 2:6 NLT

TWELVE

WHAT WOULD JESUS DO?

WWJD? What do those four letters mean to you? A past fashion craze had those four letters emblazed on wristbands and T-shirts. Was it just a marketing gimmick? Or was there something to it?

WWJD? stands for "What Would Jesus Do?" And it just may be the most powerful question you will ever answer. It's a simple question, really, but the implications are profound —and potentially life-changing.

On the most basic level, *WWJD?* can be a guide for

making decisions with moral implications. Obviously, you don't need to ask yourself, "What Would Jesus Do?" if you can't decide what to wear in the morning. But let's say you're faced with the choice between telling a lie or being truthful. When you compare your initial answer to how you think Jesus would respond, you'll either know you're doing the right thing, or you'll have a guide for change. Jesus is the perfect example because Jesus lived a perfect life. He experienced all of the pressures, temptations, and anxieties that we have, but He never did wrong.

This brings us to a deeper level of the *WWJD?* question. Even though Jesus is a perfect moral example for us, it isn't enough. Because none of us is perfect. None of us can do what Jesus did *all* the time, in every detail of our lives. We need help. More than that, we need forgiveness when we sin, which is failing to live up to God's standard of perfection. But who will help us?

In a word, Jesus. You see, even though Jesus did many things to show us how to live, He did something we could never do. He sacrificed His own life for our sins so that when we accept Jesus by faith, we satisfy God, who then gives us eternal life.

Doing what Jesus did in all situations will make you a better person here on earth. Accepting what Jesus did on the cross will secure your eternal future. Why not do both? The decision is yours.

...In the Small Stuff

- In every situation, ask yourself, "What Would Jesus Do?" Then do it.

- If you're going to compare yourself to anyone, compare yourself to Jesus. It will put your life in perspective.

- The essence of Christianity is new life in Christ. The essence of Christ is victory over death.

- Live your life in such a way that when you die even the undertaker will be sad.

- Like Jesus, if you look for the best in people, you are likely to find value in every person.

- Always do your job as if your boss were looking over your shoulder.

- Better yet, do your job as if Jesus were standing beside you.

- Jesus kept His promises until it hurt. We should do the same.

- Accept and diligently carry out the commands of those in authority over you.

- Make it your constant goal to be obedient, not victorious.

- You are less likely to fall into temptation if you don't walk along the edge.

- Deal with jealousy the moment it enters your life. Otherwise fear will come knocking.

- It's easier to change your behavior in advance than to change your reputation afterward.

- What the world sees you are, they consider Christ to be.

- As a Christian, you are designed and equipped to change the world for the glory of Jesus.

- God is looking for coordinated Christians whose walk matches their talk.

To learn,
you must
love discipline...

Proverbs 12:1 NLT

THIRTEEN

DISCIPLINE YOURSELF (NO ONE ELSE WILL)

Humans are funny beings. It used to be that many of us wanted every material thing we could get our hands on, and we wanted whatever it was to be bigger, better, or faster. Then we discovered that *outward* material things don't make us happy. So over the last few years we've turned *inward*. We've decided that it's what's inside that counts. Consequently, many of us have embarked on an inward journey, seeking to simplify our lifestyles while increasing our joy. At least that's the goal, because that's what the simplicity gurus are telling us in books like *Simple Abundance* and *Living the Simple Life*.

The idea of simplifying your life is a good one, and we'll talk more about that in Chapter 16. The problem is that we are attacking the goal with the same unbridled zest we used to collect all that stuff in the first place. Like a crazy pendulum, we swing from one extreme to the other with gusto, somehow feeling empty at both places.

So how do you find the satisfaction you've been looking for? The key is balance, consistency, and perseverance, all of which come from one thing and one thing only: *discipline.*

Here's our dilemma. We want it all, and we want it now, whether it's an abundance of possessions or an abundance of simplicity. But nothing worthwhile comes quickly, and nothing worthwhile comes without discipline. Over life's long haul, discipline works in every dimension of your life: financial, physical, mental, and spiritual. If you've ever tried to get rich quick, tried to lose weight by taking a pill, tried to get knowledge by cramming at the last minute, or attempted to get close to God by asking for a miracle, you know what we're talking about.

It's easy to get caught in the trap of quick results when you focus on the results rather than the journey. The truth is, the joy is in the journey, in the daily discipline of growing in the details of your mind, body, and spirit. The only way to bring abundance to your life—the kind of abundance that gives you joy—is to bring discipline into your life.

...In the Small Stuff

- Discipline begins with small things done daily.

- The secret behind most success stories? Discipline.

- Every morning you choose your attitude for the day.

- The first step on the path to commitment is making up your mind.

- You can plan to succeed or you can plan to fail. The choice is yours.

- Motivation increases when we assume large responsibilities with a short deadline.

- Develop a cause for your life. Whatever it is, dedicate yourself to it daily.

- Don't be good at making excuses.

- Discipline is at the heart of discipleship.

- Before diving into anything, step back and view the big picture.

- Acquire good habits; abandon bad habits.

- Move from involvement to commitment.

- Use your free time productively.

- Your dreams won't come true if you allow them to languish.

- Your dreams won't come true if you're sleeping.

- If you want to achieve excellence, begin with discipline.

- Worthwhile activities may be tough in the short-term but rewarding in the long-term.

- People will be more impressed by what you finish than by what you start.

- Motivation can fade. Habits prevail.

No, dear friends,
I am still not all I should be,
but I am focusing all my energies
on this one thing:
Forgetting the past and
looking forward to what lies ahead. . .

Philippians 3:13 NLT

FOURTEEN

Improve Yourself
(No One Else Can)

Will there ever be a time when you will stop learning and improving yourself? Will it happen when you get your high school diploma? Not then, because the education process has only just begun. At college graduation? Hardly, because the lessons of the real world await. When you become a parent with your own children to raise? Certainly not, because every parent has to stay mentally sharp just to keep up with the "new math."

Will you be able to stop learning and improving when you reach your "golden years?" That's doubtful, because then you'll need more wits than ever to figure out all of the discounts to which you are entitled.

So when does your quest to improve yourself end? When you stop breathing. Between now and then, you should consider *yourself* to be an ongoing project. A work in process. Always improving. Never stagnant.

Self-improvement is a popular topic. In the midst of our current technology generation, we are told that our minds are like computers—they are only as good as they are programmed. But the emphasis on continuing personal development is not unique to contemporary society. Several decades ago someone wrote, "You are what you think." And even before that, the Bible said, "For as he thinketh in his heart, so is he" (Proverbs 23:7 KJV).

God did not design you to be stagnant or sluggish in any respect: spiritually, physically, mentally, or socially. To borrow a book title from Chuck Swindoll, God intends that you "live above the level of mediocrity."

Self-improvement doesn't happen automatically. It requires constant, systematic, and disciplined personal development. There are books to be read, people to meet, and new places to discover. Your personal growth is a privilege, not a burden. This is where God loves to get involved in the details of your life. Let Him in and watch Him work in the small stuff of your life to help you grow and improve.

Each day, as you begin again your process of personal growth, remember that it all begins with your attitude. You must prepare your heart and program your mind for self-improvement. Like the Scripture says, "Fix your thoughts on what is true and honorable and right. Think about things that are pure and lovely and admirable. Think about things that are excellent and worthy of praise" (Philippians 4:8 NLT).

...In the Small Stuff

- Self-improvement is a lifelong process.

- Learn from the mistakes of others. You'll never live long enough to make them all yourself.

- Don't take pride in exceeding your expectations if your goals were only mediocre.

- Study and evaluate your own behavior.

- Learn to tell a good story.

- Once in a while, set a goal that absolutely terrifies you.

- Learn to thrive on challenge and change.

- When you think you've learned enough, you haven't.

- Don't be afraid to try something you don't think you can do. You may surprise yourself and you'll probably enjoy it.

- It's hard to learn from a mistake you don't acknowledge making.

- Never mistake activity for achievement.

- Develop a unique style.

- Consider how you can make a bigger impact with your time, money, and talents.

- Seeing is better than looking.

- Listening is better than hearing.

- Doing is better than talking.

Don't you know that
your body is
the temple of the Holy Spirit,
who lives in you
and was given to you by God?

1 Corinthians 6:19 NLT

FIFTEEN

Your Body Is a Temple

One of the great mysteries of our culture can be found in our obsession with physical fitness. The mystery isn't that people are exercising more. The mystery is that we're in worse shape than ever.

With the proliferation of fitness clubs, the emphasis on eating healthy foods, and the presence of at least three late-night cable shows dedicated to the latest home exercise apparatus, we should be the fittest people on the planet.

Unfortunately, *should* never got anybody into shape.

The sad truth is that we are gaining weight at an alarming rate, our children are in terrible shape, and even our professional athletes get beaten by athletes from other countries in any sport we didn't first invent.

What's the problem? We think it has to do with *intention* and *attention*. You probably have every *intention* of getting fit, but you don't. You say you're going to pay *attention* to the details of diet and exercise, but you don't. When you put those two failures together, they spell "out of shape." And out of shape usually leads to all kinds of disadvantages, such as shortness of breath, sleepiness, lack of endurance, and obesity —none of which will add years or quality to your life.

Just like every other area of your life, the secret to getting and staying healthy lies in the details. Change won't happen overnight. It takes time as a multitude of small disciplines are repeated daily. The process may be tedious, but the results are well worth the effort. Not only will you feel better, but you'll think better, too! A sound body can enhance a sound mind (conversely, health problems due to sloppy eating habits and sporadic exercise routines can undermine the mind).

We may be spiritual creatures at heart, but while we're on earth our spirits are being housed in our physical bodies. Let's do everything we can to keep the house in top shape.

...In the Small Stuff

- Fitness of the soul should take priority over fitness of the body, but the two are not mutually exclusive.

- Physical fitness should be a discipline, not an obsession.

- Consistency works better when it's linked to persistency.

- Keep in shape.

- Focus on where you are going rather than where you are.

- It's never too late to make a change in your life.

- You usually lose interest in something that's out of focus.

- When it comes to exercise, direction is more important than speed.

- If you start your day with the expectation that nothing meaningful will occur, you won't be disappointed.

- Do it now.

- What you get out of your body relates directly to what you put into it.

- Don't run with the ball unless you know the direction of the goal.

- Your biggest success will be in striving to be the best you can be, and only you can succeed at that.

- Don't go for fad diets. You may lose weight in the short term, but in the long run the only thing getting slimmer will be your wallet.

- A healthy body and a sharp mind usually go together.

- Run the race to win, even if you don't stand a chance.

This should be your ambition:
to live a quiet life,
minding your own business.

1 Thessalonians 4:11 NLT

SIXTEEN

Simplify Life and Enjoy It More

Do you long for the simple life? Many people do. It seems as if we're all too busy, have too much stuff, and owe too many bills (mainly because we have too much stuff). If you've ever said to yourself, "Stop the world, I want to get off," then you're probably a good candidate for simplicity.

But what does that mean? You may hear the word *simplicity* and right away think of self-imposed poverty or lowered ambitions. You may think of the simple life as an empty, boring existence. Think again.

Simplicity doesn't take away from your life. A simpler lifestyle may actually *add* quality and contentment to your life. When it comes to life, simplicity doesn't mean poverty. Quite the opposite, when you identify those things and those people who are really important to you, your life takes on more meaning because you pro-actively choose to do those things that will increase the quality of your life. The net result is that your life is *richer,* not poorer.

For most of us, our problem isn't that we need *more.* What we need is *better.* Do you have any things you no longer use or wear because they no longer add value to your life? Get rid of them (give them to people who don't have any stuff). Is your schedule so overloaded that you don't have time for those people and those activities that add to your life rather than taking away from it? Learn how to say "no." Learn to prioritize.

While you're giving stuff away and learning to say

no, keep this profound thought in mind: The reason our lives are so complicated is that we're too self-centered. Richard Foster writes that "simplicity means moving away from total absorption in ourselves. . .to being centered in. . . God."

God isn't the one who leads you to a more complicated life (and more stress). You get there quite well all by yourself. God wants you to give the small stuff and the stress of your life over to Him. When you trust God and let Him take the lead in your life, you will find that your life will be more peaceful and more productive. You will naturally want to clear out the clutter to make more room for God.

Thomas Kelly wrote that our deepest need "is not food and clothing and shelter, important as they are. It is God."

...In the Small Stuff

- Appreciate simplicity.

- Learn to have a good time without spending a lot of money.

- Satisfaction begins when comparison stops.

- Your needs will always outweigh your energy.

- While the poor dream of having riches, the wealthy long for simplicity.

- Anything can last more than one year.

- Don't throw money at problems.

- If you can't afford it, you don't need it.

- Never let your yearnings exceed your earnings.

- Be as satisfied with what you don't have as with what you have.

- Your wealth is measured by the fewness of your wants.

- Never buy something for the purpose of impressing others.

- Being deprived of something you desire is better than having something you despise.

- If you can't live without it, go home and sleep on it.

- Make it a lifelong goal to remove clutter.

- What you are bears little resemblance to what you have.

Your heavenly Father
already knows all your needs,
and he will give you all you need
from day to day if
you live for him and make
the Kingdom of God
your primary concern.

Matthew 6:32–33 NLT

SEVENTEEN

ARRANGE YOUR PRIORITIES

Here's an exercise that will absolutely amaze you. At the end of a day (any old day will do), sit down with a blank piece of paper and write down everything you did that day. Everything. Every detail. If you're fairly thorough (and honest), you're going to end up with a list of more than a hundred items.

Now go back and rank your activities according to the following scale, which was developed by Richard Foster:

1 – Essential
2 – Important but not essential
3 – Helpful but not necessary
4 – Trivial

When you're done, look at your list. You will see two remarkable things. First, you'll notice how many details there are in one day. How did you do all of that? Second, you'll notice how much time you spent on unnecessary and trivial things, and how little time you spent on essential and important details. Assuming you were honest, you now have a measure of your priorities, and they may not be what you expected. You thought the essential and important things were the top priorities of your life, but it's the unnecessary and even the trivial things that occupy the majority of your time.

The trouble is that the details of our lives don't really amount to much when you look at them from God's perspective. It's not that God doesn't care about our small stuff. He cares more than we do. All He asks is that we put God at the top of our priority list.

Jesus made a simple statement about priorities when He said, "Make the kingdom of God your primary concern" (Matthew 6:33 NLT). What did He mean by this? Instead of being preoccupied with the details of your life, focus on God first. Trust Him to arrange your priorities. Trust Him to handle the small stuff.

When you reduce your priorities to one detail—and it's God—then every other detail falls into place. Not right away. If this is new to you, it's going to take some time. But in a relatively short time—if you stay at it every day and give the small stuff of your life over to God—you will have a clearer and more effective focus in your life.

...In the Small Stuff

- You can start your day without God, but you'll never really get started.

- If you find yourself putting your trust in money, intelligence, beauty, or success, remember that all these things come from God. Think about where your trust really belongs.

- The way you deal with life each day depends on what you bring to life each day.

- Don't be so involved with the *when* that you miss the *now*.

- Strive to be a person of faith rather than fame.

- If what you are doing won't make a difference in five years, it probably doesn't matter now.

- You'll know something becomes meaningful when it goes from your head to your heart to your hands.

- To find out your priorities in life, look at your excesses.

- Don't let your dreams die.

- You can't plan for the future by looking in the rearview mirror.

- Whenever you look to the future, be bold.

- What you think about when you have nothing to do reveals what is important to you.

- Embrace the power of love. Reject the love of power.

- A good life is of more value than a good living.

True religion
with contentment
is great wealth.

1 Timothy 6:6 NLT

EIGHTEEN

Contentment Is Good for the Soul

Like so many words, we've lost the meaning of *contentment*. We've somehow come up with the notion that contentment is the opposite of success. We believe contentment is attainable only if we stop striving, and who wants to do that? We're afraid that if we stand still for a moment, the world is going to pass us by, so we make up our minds that we'll be contented *someday*, perhaps when we retire.

If you're an average person trying to get ahead in the world, contentment is probably the last thing you're striving for, yet there's a good chance that you *long* for it. Why? Because at its core, contentment is peace of mind. Contentment is happiness. The person who is content has little or no stress.

Yet we forge ahead like a soldier going into battle. We dive headlong into society's raging river and get caught up in a cycle of overspending, overcommitting, and overworking. And all for what? Happiness. Peace of mind. Satisfaction. But we're only kidding ourselves. Striving, consuming, and accumulating will never bring happiness. What they bring is anxiety, worry, unhappiness and—in the long run—ineffectiveness.

Even as you read this, let your mind slow down and reflect on some qualities of true contentment. First of all, being content doesn't mean being lazy. Discontentment affects the rich and poor alike. What they have in common is that they both want more stuff.

Second, don't equate contentment with being lowly or meek. There is tremendous power in contentment, because when you are content with what you have, you are free. You are free from pretense, free from concern over having it all *now*, and (in most cases) free from stress.

Third, it's not only possible but desirable to be both content and ambitious. If your ambitions come from a desire to serve God, to help others, and to improve yourself so you will have a greater impact in your world, then the fulfillment of your ambitions will bring you much happiness and contentment.

. . . In the Small Stuff

- Don't acquire everything you want.
- Contentment with your situation breeds satisfaction.

- If you believe for a moment that you own even a single possession, your contentment will be tied to it.

- If you can't get to sleep at night, check your pillow.

- If you can't get to sleep for two nights, check your mattress.

- If you can't get to sleep for three nights, check your conscience.

- Joy comes from controlling, rather than exercising, your passions.

- Consider that whatever misfortune may be your lot, someone always has it worse than you—always.

- Enjoy happiness; treasure joy.

- The best time to relax is when you're too busy.

- Beware the barrenness of a busy life.

- Cherish tranquillity.

- Since exhaustion begins and ends on the inside, that's where genuine rest must originate.

- Learn to relax without feeling guilty.

- Live somewhere between complacency and crisis.

So I tell you,
don't worry about everyday life—
whether you have enough
food, drink, and clothes.
Doesn't life consist of more
than food and clothing?

Matthew 6:25 NLT

NINETEEN

Stop Worrying and Start Living

Worrying is one of the most destructive of all human habits because it decreases your effectiveness in other areas. When you worry about something, your thoughts and your emotions focus on events that haven't yet taken place. It's like Mark Twain once said: "I am an old man and have known a great many troubles, but most of them have never happened."

Worrying is totally passive. It accomplishes nothing.

On the other hand, worrying can literally make you sick while keeping you from accomplishing the things that really matter. Here's a sobering thought: Worry can keep you from living your life the way God intended it.

Think about the things you worry about. Amazingly, you probably worry about the small stuff. Those details of life over which you have little or no control. Oswald Chambers wrote: "It is not only wrong to worry, it is unbelief; worrying means we do not believe that God can look after the practical details of our lives, and it is never anything but those details that worry us."

Jesus asked the rhetorical question, "Can all your worries add a single moment to your life? Of course not" (Matthew 6:27 NLT). If anything, worries can and will take away from your life. Are you trying to arrange the details of your life so carefully that you are leaving God out of the process? Then you're probably worrying too much. You're relying on your own abilities, and you think you have a lot to lose if things don't turn out the way you want.

Clearly the antidote to worry is trusting God to take care of the small stuff of your life. Invite Him to get involved in the details of your life. "Give all your worries and cares to God," says the Bible, "for he cares about what happens to you" (1 Peter 5:7 NLT).

...In the Small Stuff

- Live longer by worrying less.

- Don't worry about what you can't do. If you must worry, worry about why you won't do what you should do.

- Before you worry needlessly, ask yourself, "What's the worst thing that could happen?"

- When you're feeling overwhelmed, remember to take things one at a time—one day at a time.

- Worrying occurs when God is left out of the process.

- Anxiety is short-lived if we give it to God.

- If you prepare for the future, you won't have to worry about it.

- Don't worry as much about where you are as where you are going.

- Rather than worrying about change, learn to thrive on it.

- Worry is a choice.

- When you choose to worry, you are choosing not to trust God.

- Worrying can literally harm you—emotionally, physically, mentally, and spiritually.

- Instead of worrying about what you can't do, think about what God can do for you.

- The best way to stop worrying is to start praying.

- Never confuse worrying about tomorrow with planning for tomorrow.

- Prayer changes things; worry changes nothing.

Dear brothers and sisters,
whenever trouble comes your way,
let it be an opportunity for joy.
For when your faith is tested,
your endurance has
a chance to grow.

James 1:2–3 NLT

TWENTY

Embrace Adversity

Adversity is at once the greatest curse and the greatest blessing of the human race. It started in the Garden of Eden when Adam and Eve disobeyed God, who had no choice but to punish His newly created beings. God didn't curse Adam and Eve—they did that to themselves. Instead, God cursed "the ground." From that day forward, humankind has struggled to scratch a living from the earth while trying to overcome its adversity.

Oh, we're much more sophisticated these days, but

despite our technological advancements, we still fight what comes out of the ground. Whether it's big stuff like wars and weather, or smaller stuff like disease and crime, the earth and all that's in it always seem to be against us.

Of course, we humans have learned to adapt to adverse conditions fairly well. Through personal experience, each of us knows that pain and suffering are a part of life. You can't stop adversity, so you might as well deal with it. We admire people who experience extreme or continued adversity. In fact, it seems that the only path to success runs *through* adversity.

We certainly won't disagree with those who value adversity. But when we say, "embrace adversity," we're implying something quite different from what you might expect. Here's what we mean. Ever since Adam and Eve sinned and God cursed the ground, the only real blessings we have enjoyed have come from God. Even the so-called "good life" offers temporary satisfaction at best. Eventually the weeds grow in the best of gardens, and even the healthiest bodies eventually break down. In the end adversity will get the best of us.

The only person who completely defeated adversity once and for all was Jesus, and He didn't just do it for Himself. Jesus made the ultimate sacrifice by giving His own life for ours. And when we embrace what Jesus did, we are saying that only Jesus is capable and worthy of defeating our ultimate adversity—sin and death.

Go ahead and gain strength through your pain. Grow through your grief, as long as you recognize that your ability to overcome adversity is a blessing from God. As you exercise your courage, exercise your faith as well. Accept the fact that Jesus overcame adversity and now offers you rest from your own adversity and burdens.

...In the Small Stuff

- Convert your failures into successes by learning from them.

- Resist the natural inclination to hold adversity at arm's length. Embrace it willingly.

- Even when the situation seems to be at its worst, give it two more weeks.

- You will learn more from adversity than from prosperity.

- Let your difficulties be opportunities for God's control.

- God will either protect you from hardships or give you the strength to go through them. You win either way.

- A thick skin and a short memory are the best weapons against unjust criticism.

- While the prosperous people look over their shoulders with suspicion, those experiencing adversity look ahead with hope.

- Courage is not the absence of fear; it is the ability to act in the presence of fear.

- Adversity produces heartache when it comes, and exhilaration when it goes.

- You don't know you're fortunate until you're unfortunate.

- Deal creatively with adversity. When you can't pay the electric bill, have a romantic dinner by candlelight.

- Difficulties are opportunities for growth. If you try to avoid all trials, you are simply arresting your development.

He is the source
of every mercy and
the God who comforts us.

2 Corinthians 1:3 NLT

TWENTY-ONE

The God Who Comforts Us

Comfort is a rare and wonderful gift. Do you remember a time when you were a kid and you badly needed some comfort? Perhaps it was something as simple as a skinned knee, but your mother took it seriously and gave you comfort by kissing and then bandaging the hurt and telling you everything would be all right. Or maybe as you got older and someone you cared about hurt you deeply, a friend comforted you with words of encouragement.

Such memories are warm and wonderful. Yet sometimes the comfort of a loved one isn't enough. Sometimes the hurt is so deep that no human words can help relieve the pain. No mere bandage can cover the damage.

That's when you need to look beyond human comfort to something much more effective—the comfort of God. This isn't some mystical, faraway concept. God really does provide comfort to those who call upon Him in times of need. The trouble is that many people are so busy blaming God for their troubles that they don't even realize how close He is and how much He wants to comfort them. Unlike human comfort, which feels good for a moment, God's comfort supplies strength for a lifetime.

The meaning of comfort takes on significance when it describes God's actions towards us. When the Bible talks about God's comfort, it describes a comfort of strength and refreshment. At the root of God's comfort is the idea of nearness. Indeed, when He comforts us, God calls us near.

Is God calling you near in your time of trouble? Go to

Him in prayer and through His Word. There you'll find strength, safety, and solace. Are you hurting? Do you struggle with loneliness? God wants you to draw near to Him so you can feel His overwhelming love. Go ahead. Ask God for His comfort in every detail of your life.

. . . In the Small Stuff

- Looking back on what God has done for you strengthens your faith in the future.

- Even if you don't feel God is close to you, it is possible to know He is near.

- Rather than using God to solve your problems, use your problems to get closer to God.

- God doesn't promise you a life without difficulties. But He does promise that He will always be with you.

- We can't always choose the situations that life brings to us, but we can choose the attitude we will use to face them.

- Sometimes the most effective words of comfort are no words at all.

- God's comfort doesn't necessarily make you comfortable, but it will give you hope that tomorrow will be a better day.

- God may not give you comfort if it keeps you from doing what He wants you to do.

- It is possible for God to give you comfort without removing your adversity.

- God's comfort may be just what you need to deal with your adversity.

- One of the reasons God comforts us is so that we can comfort others.

- Never attach strings to the comfort you give someone else.

- If you don't know how to give comfort to others, try putting yourself in their place.

- Our ultimate comfort is knowing that someday we will be with God.

God blesses the one
who reads this prophecy
to the church,
and he blesses all
who listen to it
and obey what it says.

Revelation 1:3 NLT

TWENTY-TWO

LEARN TO READ

Someone once said that you'll be the same person five years from now as you are today except for the people you meet and the books you read. The idea is that you won't grow as a person unless you bring new (and hopefully positive) influences into your life.

The alternative is to do what most people do—nothing. They rarely or never make new friends, seek out mentors, or build into the lives of others. They rarely or never read meaningful and enriching books and articles (newspapers, gossip magazines, and posts to a stranger's Facebook page don't count).

Don't get us wrong. We're not saying that you should dump your old friends in favor of some new ones (unless you're running around with a bunch of losers). And we're not saying you should avoid all things frivolous when you read. We're just issuing you a challenge to step up your friendships and your reading habits to the next level.

Reading is the gateway for growth. Books contain information, insight, and inspiration—all of which contribute significantly to your mental and spiritual development. Without the guidance of books, you're guessing at best. You're like a boat at sea without compass or map: You have the power to get somewhere but you have no direction.

Books contain the experiences of people who have failed miserably as well as those who have achieved greatly (both are useful). Good books also present ideas and concepts that stretch beyond our self-imposed limits.

This is especially true with the Bible. The greatest book

ever written will teach, correct, inspire, and point you to the Author. King David wrote that the words of God are "more desirable than gold" and "sweeter than honey" (Psalm 19:10 NLT). The Bible is the basic guide for life. Read it daily. And make it a habit to read other enriching books as well.

. . .In the Small Stuff

- The person who does not read good books has no advantage over the person who can't read them.

- Build your personal library with hard cover books that will transcend centuries and circumstances.

- Read the front page of a local newspaper every day. Keep up on current events.

- Read for fifteen minutes every night before you go to bed.

- The history of the world is merely the biography of great people.

- Read at least one biography a year.

- Read *How to Win Friends and Influence People* by Dale Carnegie at least once a year.

- Be a reader, but one who reads between the lines.

- At the beginning of each year, choose a topic of interest and spend the next twelve months learning all you can about it.

- Try reading the handwriting on the wall before your back is up against it.

- Next time you read a really great book, make every effort to get in touch with the author.

- Reading books on a variety of subjects broadens your personal knowledge and appeal.

- Read one book a month.

- Reward your kids every time they read a book.

- Just because it's in print does not make it worth reading.

- Just because it's on TV does not make it worth watching.

- Listen to books on tape in the car.

- Try doing without TV for a week.

- Every time you read a book by a new author, go back and read a classic that has stood the test of time.

Your lives are a letter
written in our hearts,
and everyone can read it
and recognize our good work among you.

2 Corinthians 3:2 NLT

TWENTY-THREE

Learn to Write

Many people like to read, but few enjoy writing. That's probably because most of our writing experiences have centered around undesirable projects, such as research papers in school. And unlike reading a book, there's no such thing as "skimming" your writing. There are no shortcuts.

Another reason why people are reluctant to write is that they're afraid someone else is going to read what they've written. When you get past writing for a grade in school, you develop a self-consciousness. Maybe you can't get past the idea that someone's going to "grade" you for spelling and grammar. Maybe you're afraid someone will criticize—or worse—laugh at what you've written (especially when it's not supposed to be funny).

So you rarely write and you miss out on one of the greatest forms of communication and self-expression. Here's a fact. When you express yourself through writing, you reveal more about yourself than you ever could by talking, even if you aren't writing about yourself. Writing forces you to choose your words more carefully because it forces you to think more deeply.

We want to help you begin a personal writing career. Forget about becoming the next great American novelist or even getting anything published (although we'd be the last to discourage you). What we have in mind is personal writing—also known as *journaling*—that may never be read by another soul (okay, the pressure's off).

Here's an easy way to start a journal. Buy one of those blank books (all the bookstores carry them) and begin jotting down your *feelings* about stuff. Write down the details of your life and then tell yourself how they are affecting you. Don't worry about grammar or spelling. Just write.

Write how you feel about the people in your life. Write how you feel about God. For inspiration in this area, read the Psalms, which contain some of the most personal and passionate writing in the Bible. If you take a little time a few times each week to jot down your thoughts, you will be amazed at the results. You will find that the small stuff in your life will feel more ordered, and the big stuff won't seem so imposing.

...In the Small Stuff

- Learn to write fascinating letters.
- Write a thank you note to a teacher from your past

- A handwritten note beats a typed one every time.

- Develop your vocabulary, but don't overuse fancy words.

- Write an autobiography and update it annually.

- Here's a tip for the next time you write one of those Christmas letters nobody reads: Make up a bunch of stuff and see if anybody calls.

- Develop your vocabulary to express yourself, not to impress others.

- Imitate your life insurance agent: Be systematic about sending birthday cards to people who are important to you.

- Everybody has a life story. Think about yours, write it down, and then look for an opportunity to relate it publicly.

- If you enjoy expressing yourself with words, try writing more and talking less.

- Get into the habit of writing thank you notes, even for little things or acts of kindness.

- When you write, use short sentences and descriptive words.

- After you've written something, go back and read it out loud. You'll become a better writer.

- One of the best ways to develop a good writing style is to read good books.

Dear friends,
be quick to listen,
slow to speak,
and slow to get angry.

James 1:19 NLT

TWENTY-FOUR

Communication Is More Than Talking

When it comes to communication, there are two kinds of people in the world—those who love to hear others talk, and those who love to hear themselves talk (and we all know which kinds of people are more fun to be with).

Good communication skills begin with listening. Not only do you learn things about other people by listening, but you also make others feel important when you give them your full attention, complete with head nods and eye contact. Of course, your goal may be to help others become good listeners by doing all the talking yourself. While we don't recommend this, we do offer this word of advice: Learn to distinguish between head nods that show genuine interest and those that indicate that your listener is dozing off out of sheer boredom.

If you're still not convinced that listening is a better communication skill than talking, try this experiment. The next time you're with a bunch of people at a party or special event, do your best to listen intently. Stroke your chin and say, "I see," when someone makes a point. Occasionally squint your eyes and go, "Mmmm," when another person says something interesting. Ask questions rather than make statements.

If you keep this up, we guarantee that at the end of the evening you will be considered by everyone else to be the most thoughtful and dynamic person in the room. You will also appear incredibly wise.

Even if you don't aspire to become a world-class listener, you can always improve your communications skills by self-editing your conversations. Keep talking, but use fewer words (*better* words, too). Avoid the extremes of empty flattery and harmful gossip (what other kind of gossip is there?).

Here's another form of nonverbal communication that's extremely effective. Whenever someone has done something nice for you, write a thank you note. When someone needs a lift, write a personal note of encouragement. When tragedy strikes another, express your sympathy with a heartfelt card. You'll never know how meaningful your written words will be to others.

...In the Small Stuff

- People are attracted to enthusiasm.

- Have a ready smile and a firm handshake.

- Be the first one to ask a question.

- Think about your question before you ask it.

- A wink delivers a powerful message, so be careful at whom you wink.

- A card sent with a personal note inside is more meaningful than a card sent but only signed.

- Develop exceptional listening habits.

- Listen with your eyes as well as your ears.

- Sometimes it's easiest to communicate face-to-face if you're walking side by side.

- No one will ever accuse you of being a boring conversationalist if you let people talk about themselves.

- A truly eloquent speech includes all that is necessary—and no more.

- Thoughtful compliments wear better than impulsive flattery.

- You learn more by listening (you already know what *you* would say).

- Use superlatives sparingly.

- People who talk a lot about themselves seldom want to hear what others have to say.

So encourage each other
and build each other up. . .

1 Thessalonians 5:11 NLT

TWENTY-FIVE

Encouragement Is a Gift

People seldom think of encouragement as a gift because it seems so ordinary. But it isn't. Encouragement is actually quite rare (because it's seldom given) and it is valuable (because it's so meaningful to the recipient). In our humble opinion, encouragement makes the perfect gift, and here's why:

It's free. Encouraging someone requires absolutely no cash outlay. This doesn't mean there is no cost. It may cost you time, creativity, and thoughtfulness. But all of that is what makes encouragement so appreciated. It requires something from *you*, not just something from your wallet.

It requires no shopping. You don't have to make a trip to the mall for this gift. Many times the gift can be delivered from your home or office. Writing a note of support or making an encouraging phone call may be all that's necessary.

It doesn't have to be gift-wrapped. Attractive wrapping adds to the appeal of a gift, but none is needed with encouragement. It is beautiful all by itself.

It can be custom-designed. You don't have to worry about sizes. But you must still give some thought to making your gift of encouragement a perfect fit. You have to think about some details—what are the best words of comfort, motivation, or support the person needs to hear.

It doesn't require batteries. So many gifts require batteries as an energy source. Not so with encouragement. It creates energy all by itself. If you don't think so, just watch the increase in activity when you motivate someone with a kind and supportive comment.

It will last a lifetime. Think about it. What other gift could you give to a child that will have value years later? Encouragement can do just that. A little word can make a big difference, and the results can be life-changing.

Oh, there's one more thing about encouragement. No one ever gets too much of it. So don't be stingy. Give it often.

...In the Small Stuff

- Enthusiasm encourages positive behavior.

- Ask for advice often. Offer advice sparingly.

- Be kind to unkind people. It gets to them.

- Encouragement, praise, and recognition are often more effective than a raise or bonus, and they're always cheaper.

- Love first if you long to be loved.

- You will encourage more people by listening than by talking.

- A pleasant expression increases your face value.

- Personal happiness is most easily gained by bringing happiness to others.

- Criticism becomes constructive when you make it a challenge.

- Avoid making statements that can be taken two ways.

- It's a joy to steer heavenward someone who's been going south.

- Be happy for others in their good fortune.

- Never expect gratitude, but always express appreciation.

- You can't always control the kind of service you receive, but you can always control the kind of gratitude you deliver.

- Compliment people as soon as it occurs to you.

- Just as you can have false modesty, you can encourage insincerely. Learn to be a *sincere* encourager.

- Encourage those who look up to you.

- Make it a habit to encourage youngsters.

———————

If God has given
you leadership ability,
take the responsibility seriously.

———————

Romans 12:8 NLT

TWENTY-SIX

LEADERSHIP IS AN ART

There are as many sayings about leadership as there are leadership styles. The forceful leader says, "Lead, follow, or get out of the way." The reluctant leader says, "Lead by example." The business leader says, "A great leader puts his vision into action." There is some truth in all of these leadership models, but none of these concepts hits the bull's-eye of leadership. To do that we have to go to the greatest leader ever, the person who has impacted more people and changed more lives for the better than anyone else—Jesus Christ.

Jesus never wrote a book on leadership. He was never elected to public office and never ran a company. Although Jesus once spoke to more than five thousand people (before giving them a free lunch), He focused His attention on twelve ordinary men. He really preferred to relate to people one at a time.

Just because Jesus never hit the motivational speaking circuit or traveled more than a hundred miles from his hometown doesn't mean He didn't address the core values of leadership. In fact, Jesus was very concerned about leaders and leadership, because He knew His followers would have to carry on His teachings long after He was gone.

One of the last things Jesus said to His followers concerned leadership. He told them, "Those who are the greatest should take the lowest rank, and the leader should be like a servant" (Luke 22:26 NLT).

There you have it. The greatest leadership principle ever from the greatest leader ever. If you want to lead, you have to serve. If you want to be the leader of many people, you have to serve many people. There are many examples of leaders who are ruthless, self-serving, and greedy. You can find them in business, in government, and in families. But such leaders ultimately fail to let God into the details of their lives. They shut Him out completely while trying to manage their little kingdoms.

If you want to be a great leader in God's Kingdom—the only one that counts for eternity—then you need to let God into the small stuff of your life as you faithfully serve others.

...In the Small Stuff

- Empowering is more effective than delegating.

- Have the courage to hold people accountable.

- Associate with leaders as often as you can. When you're around them, carry a note pad and write things down.

- A signpost, like a peer, only warns you about the road ahead. But a map, like a mentor, can show you how to get where you want to go.

- Find a mentor.

- Being a good example is better than giving good advice.

- An exceptional leader is one who gets average people to do superior work.

- There are born leaders and there are leaders who are made. And then there are those who become leaders out of necessity.

- If you want to lead, read.

- When you find a leader, follow.

- When you identify a follower, lead.

- Use your influence sparingly. It will last longer.

- Be available to take someone's place in an emergency.

- Power begins to corrupt the moment you begin to seek it.

- Managing people begins with caring for them.

- One of the sobering characteristics of leadership is that leaders are judged to a greater degree than followers.

You cannot serve both
God and money.

Luke 16:13 NLT

TWENTY-SEVEN

Money:
Learn to Deal with It

What is it about money that causes business partnerships to dissolve, friendships to break apart, and marriages to end? More accurately, what is it about money that motivates people to turn against each other?

As usual, the answer to this crucial question can be found in the Bible. Actually, money is a major topic in the Bible. Jesus frequently talked about money because He knew that its most damaging effect is to keep people away from

God. He once said, "It is very hard for a rich person to get into the Kingdom of Heaven" (Matthew 19:23 NLT).

The reason why money makes us greedy is because we want it so much. And the reason why money can keep us away from God is because we're afraid we're going to lose it. Jesus addressed this incredible human tendency toward blatant stupidity (if rejecting eternal life with God for the temporary pleasures of money isn't stupidity, we don't know what is) when He said, "How do you benefit if you gain the whole world but lose or forfeit your own soul in the process?" (Luke 9:25 NLT). Good question. So why do we do what we do when it comes to money? Why do we work so hard to get it and then work even harder to keep it?

We think it has something to do with *ownership*. If there's one quality we humans value above all others, it's self-reliance. And there's nothing that demonstrates self-reliance more than ownership. We love to own stuff because we love the feeling of controlling the details of our lives. It doesn't matter if you're running a multinational corporation or cashing your checks at Paychecks Plus each week; you love the feeling that money gives you.

There's only one way to release money's grip on our lives, and that's to give up the idea of ownership. We've got to realize that God is the real owner of everything we have. No, He doesn't need all your stuff (hey, *you* don't even need all your stuff), but He does want your heart. He wants you to let Him into the details of your life—especially all your stuff—so He can lift you to a higher level of living. "After all," wrote the apostle Paul, "we didn't bring anything with us when we came into the world, and we certainly cannot carry anything with us when we die" (1 Timothy 6:7 NLT).

At best, our job is to manage what God has blessed us with. In fact, that's why God put us on this planet in the first place—to manage *His* stuff, which includes His rivers, seas, plants, animals, and resources.

Don't get us wrong. God doesn't want you to be foolish with His money. Live wisely and share with those in need. Above all, seek God and His Kingdom first, and He'll provide for everything you need.

...In the Small Stuff

- Manage your money as if it belongs to God (it does).

- If your outgo exceeds your income, your upkeep will be your downfall.

- Watch the pennies and the dollars will take care of themselves.

- Budget your future. Don't outlive your money.

- There is little benefit to acquiring wealth if you fail at managing it.

- Set aside money each month for Christmas.

- From every dollar you earn save some and tithe some.

- Use a credit card only if you can pay the bill in full at the end of the month.

- The time to worry about money is before you spend it.

- Instead of valuing something by its cost, figure out how much it's worth.

- A vacation is more enjoyable if you stay within your budget.

- Set aside money each month for vacations.

- You aren't living within your means if you have to borrow money to do it.

- Let money be your servant, not your master.

The generous prosper
and are satisfied;
those who refresh others
will themselves be refreshed.

Proverbs 11:25 NLT

TWENTY-EIGHT

A GENEROUS SPIRIT WORKS WONDERS

The greatest cure for greed is generosity. It's also one of the most satisfying feelings in the world. We're not talking about giving your old clothes to the Salvation Army (the only thing you'll probably feel by doing that is the satisfaction of cleaning out your closet). The only way to feel the satisfaction of true generosity is to give away something you value.

This takes generosity beyond money to a realm that

includes both possessions and time. That's what the apostle Paul meant when he wrote that we should "be rich in good works and should give generously to those in need, always being ready to share with others whatever God has given them" (1 Timothy 6:18 NLT).

The spirit of generosity has become rather stylish in recent years, and that's probably a good thing. The danger in popularizing generosity is that some people may want to publicize their giving. When that happens, you have to wonder about the true motive. There's also the issue of giving out of your abundance as opposed to giving sacrificially. Both kinds of giving can be useful, but only one gets God's attention.

When it comes to generosity, ask yourself two questions. First, does your generosity come from your heart? A truly generous person gives out of love and compassion, not from a desire to impress others. You also want to give cheerfully, not grumpily. Generosity is incompatible with criticism, resentment, or regret.

Here's another question to ask. Is your generosity productive? In other words, are you giving money, stuff, or time away without accepting responsibility for the consequences? Don't be foolish. Pay attention to the details of where your giving is going. Remember, each time you give to those "in need," you are making an investment of God's resources. Invest wisely. Be a good money manager by making sure your generosity is productive.

...In the Small Stuff

- Money is like fertilizer: It's not much good unless it's spread around.

- If you want to be needy—hoard.

- If you want to be poor—grasp.

- If you want to be rich—give.

- Think of your net worth as what you have given rather than what you have.

- Give money to people or organizations you can stay personally involved with.

- Initiative is seeing what needs to be done and doing it before you are asked.

- Filling an existing need can be as valuable as anticipating a new one.

- Give the gift of time. It's a gift more valuable than money can buy.

- Giving is more fulfilling when you align it with your interests and goals.

- The measure of your success is not what is in your wallet but what is in your heart.

- Support a missionary financially.

- When you give a gift, expect nothing in return.

- Generosity does not include giving away something you'll never miss.

- The more specific you make your giving, the more productive it will be.

- Before you financially support an individual or an organization, find out if the following characteristics are evident: purpose, strategy, and accountability.

- Share your blessings with others.

- The generous person always has more than enough; the greedy person never has enough.

If you think you are
too important to help
someone in need,
you are only fooling yourself.
You are really a nobody.

Galatians 6:3 NLT

TWENTY-NINE

Compassion:
Much More Than Pity

It's possible to be a generous person and still lack compassion for others. Here's how it works. Let's say a young man came to your door asking you to purchase some candy or magazine subscriptions for a youth program of some sort, and you know he doesn't live in your neighborhood. Someone has dropped him off to canvass the homes on your street.

Even though this young man is well-mannered and

has obviously done a good job of memorizing a little speech, you have doubts. You wonder if you should give him $15 for the candy or the magazines. But you feel a sense of obligation, or you feel a bit guilty for turning others away before, or maybe you feel sorry for the young man—so you reluctantly agree to make a purchase.

Have you been generous? Perhaps. Did you pity the young man? Maybe. But there's one thing you didn't have, and that's compassion.

Simply giving something away—whether it's your money or your time—doesn't necessarily mean you have compassion for someone else. Never make the mistake of equating generosity with compassion. If anything, a generous spirit flows from your compassion, not the other way around. True compassion means that you see other people the way God sees them. It means looking into the heart of these people that God, for one reason or another, brings into your life.

These people may be complete strangers, or they may

be people you've known—or least known about—for years. They all have one thing in common: they are loved equally by God, who made them in His image.

C. S. Lewis wrote that there are no *ordinary* people. "You have never talked to a mere mortal." Human beings are the only living creatures with an immortal soul. "Next to the Blessed Sacrament," Lewis wrote, "your neighbor is the holiest object presented to your senses."

Who is your neighbor? Anyone in need, whether the need is physical or spiritual. True compassion reaches out to your neighbor. That young man on your porch is your neighbor, and true compassion reaches out and treats him with respect as one of God's beloved. And true compassion expresses itself with a kind word of encouragement, a cool cup of water, and sometimes the purchase of a box of candy.

...In the Small Stuff

- Let your primary motivation be the still small voice of the Holy Spirit.

- Don't wait to do one great thing for God in your lifetime. Rather, do many good little things for the sake of His kingdom, which in itself is a great thing.

- Get to know your intuitions; God may be speaking to you.

- What happens to you may be an accident. How you respond is not.

- Make sure your caring includes doing.

- No one does the right thing naturally. It takes effort and practice.

- Help the helpless and give to the needy, but do it out of compassion, not pity.

- Passion and compassion are closely related.

- Feeling good about yourself begins with serving others.

- Your care for others is a measure of your greatness.

We were filled with laughter,
and we sang for joy.

Psalm 126:2 NLT

THIRTY

LAUGH AND THE WORLD LAUGHS WITH YOU

You've heard it said that laughter is the best medicine. Well, it may not be the *best* prescription for what ails you, but it is beneficial for your health. Medical researchers have determined that laughter has a profound and instantaneous effect on virtually every important organ in the human body. Best of all, laughter reduces tension as it relaxes the tissues.

At great expense, people join health clubs for cardiovascular exercise. Laughter can produce similar results at far less cost. It stirs up the blood, expands the chest, electrifies the nerves, and clears the brain. Laughter provides refreshment to the entire body.

Abraham Lincoln understood the benefits of laughter when he said, "With the fearful strain that is on me night and day, if I did not laugh I should die."

If you aren't a laugher, become one. Try it. You'll enjoy it. And if you're having trouble finding something to laugh at, start with yourself. Many people are too impressed with themselves to enjoy their humanity. They are missing out on some great laughs.

Laughing at ourselves gives us a more accurate sense of who we are. It breaks down barriers between others and us. It makes us more approachable. It projects a personality that is warm and friendly instead of rigid and stuffy. Laughter is like a magnet that attracts people. And if you can learn to laugh at yourself, you are guaranteed to have a lifetime of amusement.

Make your home a place that is filled with laughter. That won't be difficult if you look for humor in the small stuff of life. Start with the family photo album. Laughter shared between parents and children is more effective than any curfew. It is a guaranteed formula for producing well-adjusted children. A child who knows how to enjoy laughter is better equipped to handle life as an adult.

Laughter is the secret to a long and enjoyable life. People don't stop laughing because they grow old. They grow old because they stop laughing. He who laughs, lasts.

...In the Small Stuff

- Our five senses are incomplete without the sixth—a sense of humor.

- Suppress neither sneezes nor laughter.

- Remember the punch line before you tell the joke.

- The best jokes are painless and profaneless.

- Laugh at yourself. Laugh with others.

- You know you have a good sense of humor if you can laugh when someone tells your joke better than you.

- Laugh at yourself as much as others do.

- A true sense of humor does not rely on the humiliation of others.

- Leave funny and enthusiastic messages on answering machines and voice mail.

- If you can laugh at yourself, you are guaranteed a lifetime of chuckling.

- If someone tells you a joke you've already heard, let them finish and laugh anyway.

- There's a time to be serious and a time to laugh. Learn to tell the difference.

- Develop the art of telling stories that are short, clean, and funny.

- If you doubt that God has a sense of humor, look in the mirror.

- Humor works best when it brings joy to others.

Stop judging others,
and you will not be judged.
For others will treat you
as you treat them.

Matthew 7:1–2 NLT

THIRTY-ONE

CRITICIZE AND YOU WALK ALONE

Jesus made a memorable statement about criticism when He compared it to pointing out a piece of sawdust in someone else's eye while ignoring the log sticking out of your own eye.

Criticism always focuses on picky little things. Small stuff. We take something that bugs us about someone else —no matter how small—and blow it all out of proportion (this is especially true of the people closest to us). Rarely is our criticism constructive.

The truth is that we don't criticize others in order to help them. We criticize in order to make ourselves feel more important. We end up exaggerating the faults of others while excusing or ignoring our own shortcomings.

If we're going to focus on the small stuff in anybody's life, it ought to be our own. We're not advocating morbid introspection, which can lead to all kinds of abnormal behavior, but honest self-evaluation. Ben Franklin (the American statesman, not the five-and-dime guy) used to keep a list of virtues—such as honesty, thriftiness, courage, and kite-flying—that he wanted in his life, and every day he evaluated himself to see how he measured up.

Honest self-evaluation is really nothing more than letting God into the details of your life, whether it's your stuff or your personality. When you do this you open yourself up to self-improvement. Here's what's going to happen: God will bring to your consciousness an awareness of areas where you need to improve; He will speak to you through His Word (as you read it, of course); and God will use people to give you honest (and sometimes painful) evaluations of your behavior.

Through all of these ways you will discover what God desires from you. And you will be less likely to criticize others.

...In the Small Stuff

- People of low ambition are overly critical because so much in life is beyond their reach.

- Motivate, don't denigrate.

- Listening to gossip is as wrong as spreading it.

- Gossip should never be disguised as concern.

- "I'm sorry." Two words with unlimited potential.

- If you agree to bury the hatchet, don't leave the handle sticking out.

- Criticism and success are both difficult to handle, but one is ultimately more enjoyable.

- Never criticize your hair cutter—at least not while yours is the hair being cut.

- Criticism and finding fault are not spiritual gifts.

- A word spoken in anger cannot be erased. It plays over and over again.

- Walk on soles, not on souls.

- Be generous with praise and stingy with criticism.

- To belittle is to be little.

- Appreciate differences instead of criticizing them.

- The urge to criticize someone usually comes from feelings of resentment.

- If you make an effort to overlook the little faults in others, they'll do the same for you.

- Rather than taking criticism personally, look at it objectively.

- Learn to distinguish between constructive and destructive criticism.

- It's okay to give constructive criticism if it's done in love.

- It's impossible to offer destructive criticism and love someone at the same time.

Don't just pretend that you love others. Really love them. . . . Love each other with genuine affection, and take delight in honoring each other.

Romans 12:9–10 NLT

THIRTY-TWO

Relationships Take Time

One hundred years ago, our society was influenced greatly by the farm culture. That lifestyle was slower. There was a season for planting, a season for growing, and a season for harvesting. There was a natural pattern and timetable for living which couldn't be rushed.

Today we live in a technological society where things can't happen fast enough. Everything is instant—from oatmeal to news. Everything is fast—from food to faxes. We even get frustrated when it takes a few extra milliseconds for the computer to warm up. Our society is characterized by words like: "over-nite", "drive-thru", and "log-on". We get impatient with anything that takes time.

There is one aspect of life which cannot be rushed—building a meaningful relationship with another person. You can make an acquaintance "on the spot," but a friendship won't happen instantaneously. And it doesn't develop overnight. It takes *time*. The most precious commodity of our "hurry up" society must be invested over the long-term if you expect to have a friendship that is dependable and fulfilling.

Growing a friendship is not unlike growing a crop. There has to be a season of *planting*: Time is spent in finding common interests. These initial contacts are followed by a season of *growing*: The friendship is nurtured beyond common interests as you begin to appreciate each other's differences which are discovered only by spending time together. As the relationship matures, you can begin a lifelong season of *harvest*: This is when the friendship proves to be a source of strength and encouragement to you.

We all want meaningful friendships. We desire relationships which are based on trust and loyalty, those which go beyond shallow courtesy all the way to "do anything for each other" commitments. You can have this kind of friendship, but it will take time. Your time.

...In the Small Stuff

- There are many areas in your life that require constant maintenance: your yard, your garage, your house, your relationships.

- When someone does something good for you, never forget it.

- When you do something good for someone else, let it go immediately.

- Be quick to receive the truth, and even quicker to dismiss gossip.

- Be a peacemaker.

- You can tell a little about a person by what he says about himself.

- You can tell a lot about a person by what others say about him.

- You can tell even more by what he says about others.

- Ask questions.

- A smile is your most important accessory.

- Examine your life for the faults you find most irritating in others.

- Commit yourself to projects; dedicate yourself to people.

- Do something for someone without taking credit.

- Spend more of your time, energy, and resources investing in people than you do investing in things.

- Associate with people who lift you up.

- Disassociate with people who pull you down.

- Seek out quiet people. They have a lot to say.

This is the message
we have heard
from the beginning:
We should love one another.

1 John 3:11 NLT

THIRTY-THREE

HOW TO REALLY LOVE YOUR SPOUSE

There are four ways to love your spouse (now would be a good time to review Chapter 3). But only one way will keep your marriage together.

You can have affection for your spouse. You can consider your spouse your best friend. And your sex life can be so great that Dr. Phil wants to hear all about it. In fact, it's possible to have all three of these feelings for your spouse, which is great. There's only one problem. Feelings come and go, especially in a marriage. One day you and your spouse are best friends, and the next day you can't stand each other. It happens. And marriages fall apart because couples base the whole thing on feelings.

Which brings us to the fourth love, the one love that will keep your marriage together, as long as both of you take it to heart. It's that love with the funny name—*agape* love—which is the love that desires the best for the other person. This is unselfish love that seeks to give rather than take. This is love that takes work.

Here's another way to look at it: *Love is in the details.* For a husband this means paying attention to the small stuff. It means remembering and planning special celebrations for anniversaries and birthdays (hint: she loves flowers, dinner, and weekends away). It means helping around the house, especially if your wife has a career outside the home. And it means (okay, guys, here's a tough one) actually sitting down and having meaningful, interactive conversations.

For a wife, *love is in the details* means showing interest

in his work and hobbies. It means taking a breath between sentences so you can hear what he's thinking, even if he merely grunts (learn to interpret his grunts—there are many shades of meaning). And it means offering your support and encouragement (let's face it, your husband is more insecure than he lets on—all men are).

If loving your spouse unselfishly is a challenge for you, think about the way Jesus loves you. The Bible says that Jesus willingly "made himself nothing" in order to completely serve those He loved. And now He asks you to love your spouse in the same sacrificial way.

...In the Small Stuff

- Loving your spouse is not enough. Learn how to demonstrate your love.

- Compliment your spouse with elegant words.

- Forgiveness is at the heart of love.

- Think back and remember one thing you really admired about your spouse when you were dating.

- Plan one romantic getaway a year with your spouse.

- Make a date to go out to dinner with your spouse at least once a month.

- Tell your spouse "I love you" at least once a day. Say it all the time with your eyes.

- Celebrate your spouse's birthday, but hold the relish to tell jokes about age.

- Be as enthusiastic to stay married as you were to get married.

- Remember when you got married.

- Remember where you got married.

- Remember why you got married.

- Be loyal to your spouse. Express admiration in public.

- A marriage can be a great investment that yields tremendous dividends, if you have the interest.

- Give your spouse a gift for no reason.

- If you express your love to your spouse often enough, you'll never have to ask if your spouse loves you.

- Trade in your car, not your spouse.

- Embrace your spouse.

Children are
a gift from the Lord;
they are a reward from him.

Psalm 127:3 NLT

THIRTY-FOUR

THE PERFECT GIFT FOR YOUR YOUNG CHILD

There is no shortage of gift ideas for your young child. Millions of advertising dollars are devoted to directing your attention to the "perfect" gift. You feel guilty if you can't find something that will educate, stimulate, and build self-esteem all at once (and it's got to be politically correct, biodegradable, and bilingual, too). The marketers know that price is no object because this is *your* child, and you won't settle for anything less than the best.

Well, we have a suggestion for the perfect gift. It is not easy to find, and it is terribly expensive, but we guarantee that it will last a lifetime and it will be your child's favorite. We're talking about your *time*.

Your child's greatest need is the security of knowing that you care. There is no better way to convey your love than to spend time with your child. Hours invested in your child will produce dividends now and in the future. You will be building a relationship, moment by moment, that will be the basis for a lifelong friendship between the two of you.

Don't be misled by the myth of "quality time"—it is an admirable goal, but it should not be used as an excuse for missing "quantity time" with your child. Quality moments usually can't be scheduled. They happen spontaneously, without warning, in circumstances you don't anticipate. Those precious, teachable moments will be initiated by your child, while you're playing in the backyard, driving in the car, or staring at a worm in the dirt. For your children, all of the time you spend together can be "quality time" because it is then that they have what's most important to them—your attention.

This is a gift which does not come cheaply. It will cost you. You may have to forgo other activities. You will have to say "no" to other people. You may have to set aside a few personal goals or hobbies for a few years. But don't worry. Those other things and folks will be around later, but the childhood years are soon gone forever. They are irretrievable.

Give your child the gift of your time. Sure, there is a limited supply, but we've never seen a tombstone which read: "I wish I hadn't spent so much time with my kids."

...In the Small Stuff

- Teach your children to do more than they are asked to do.

- Help your child to discover his or her God-given abilities—then develop them.

- Speak with your children, not at them.

- Sit with your children, not on them.

- Teach your children by your words (make sure they are kind), by your actions (make sure they are wholesome), and by your temperament (make sure it is controlled).

- True education must begin by instilling honesty in your children.

- Teach your kids responsibility early.

- Let your kids help you plan your next vacation.

- When you talk to your children, get to their level and look them in the eye.

- Hug your kids.

- Take your kids out for ice cream after they've performed in sports, drama, or music, especially if they didn't do very well.

- Attend every open house at your children's schools.

- Don't miss these "firsts" in your child's life: the first word spoken, the first steps taken, the first day of school, the first graduation, the first game won, the first game lost, the first big heartbreak, the first big success.

- Kiss your kids good night every evening, even it if wakes them up.

Teach your children
to choose the right path,
and when they are older,
they will remain upon it.

Proverbs 22:6 NLT

THIRTY-FIVE

How to Really Love Your Teenager

Every teenage generation since the 1960s has been distrustful of adults and marked with an attitude of rebellion. You can hear it in their music. You can see it in the way they dress. Their attitude is entirely understandable, however, if you consider the world from their perspective. Their governmental leaders are hypocrites, saying whatever is politically expedient; their sports heroes prove to be egocentric millionaires who can't sign an autograph for a kid without a fee; and their religious leaders fall in disgrace because their lives fail to match the content of their sermons. In short, teenagers are quick to criticize what adults tolerate: The world is full of role models who are phonies and fakes.

If you have a child who is a teenager, then set an example which your child can follow. These are easy words to say, but they are difficult to fulfill. No one knows you better than your teenager. No one sees you so often and in so many different circumstances. Good days and bad days. At work and at play. At ease and under stress. Your teenager is there: watching and analyzing; seeing if your actions match your words.

For your teenager, your words are not trustworthy until your actions are found to be so.

- Do you want your child to learn the meaning of honesty? Then be honest yourself. Admit to making a mistake; acknowledge that you don't know all of the answers (because your teenager already suspects that you are bluffing); and don't cover up your own shortcomings.

- Do you want your teenager to have moral character? Then don't make promises unless you know you can keep them. Be just and equitable in establishing the rules of the household. Don't require any behavior from your child that you don't consistently exhibit yourself.

You already are an example for your teenager—whether you intend to be or not. The question is what *kind* of an example. Don't just *talk* to your teenager about life; show what you mean by how you live.

...In the Small Stuff

- If your kids don't stand for something, they'll fall for anything.

- Every teenager should know that choices determine consequences.

- Some adversity is simply the result of bad choices.

- Compliment a teenager as soon as it occurs to you.

- Make your home a place where your kids can bring their friends.

- Tell your kids they have a special future and then do all you can to help them realize their dreams.

- Ask your teenager to name his or her heroes. You'll probably be surprised.

- There is a delicate balance between respecting your children's privacy and knowing what's going on in their lives.

- Know the difference between tolerance and permissiveness.

- Fight the natural tendency to talk rather than listen to your teenager.

- There are those who experience joy and terror simultaneously. Ask a parent whose teenager has just obtained a driver's license.

- Encourage your kids to develop their own style.

- Convince your kids that there's more to life than fast food.

- The next rainy day, show your kids their baby pictures.

———————

I could have no greater joy
than to hear that
my children live
in the truth.

———————

3 John 4 NLT

THIRTY-SIX

When Your Child Leaves Home

Perhaps you have survived the progression of your child from diapers to diploma. During that time, it was your child who made most of the changes. Now it is *your* turn because your child's entry into adulthood will require major adjustments to your role as a parent. You spent almost two decades as a "hands-on" manager of your child's life. That time is over. Get ready to be an "outside consultant."

Once away from home, your child lives independently

without any obligation of accountability to you. How do you convey your interest and concern without being accused of meddling? Here are a few suggestions:

Keep checking in without checking up. You are curious about what is going on in your child's life. There is nothing wrong with that. But make sure that your child realizes that your curiosity is heartfelt and not judgmental. After all, your child is responsible for his or her own actions, and there will be resentment if you are perceived as monitoring.

Learn to listen instead of lecture. Be quick to listen and slow to speak. You want to create a relationship which fosters communication. This won't happen if every conversation ends with a scolding.

Give advice only when asked. You are painfully aware that your child still has much to learn, and you have an extra generation of experience from which your child can benefit. Unfortunately, your child may not realize this obvious fact at first. But hang in there. Sooner or later, after exhausting his or her own resources, you may be thrilled to hear, "What do you think I should do?"

Ask questions for the sake of praying, not prying. Forget the litany of "who, what, when" interrogation techniques you developed when your child was a teenager. Shift to more generic inquiries, such as "How would you like me to be praying for you?"

Your love for your child doesn't diminish when he or she becomes an adult and leaves home. But the way in which you interact with your child will be drastically different. Appreciate the difference. Your child certainly will.

...In the Small Stuff

- Spend time with your kids now, and they'll spend time with you later.

- You will have no greater joy than to hear that your children walk in truth.

- Be more concerned with the heritage you'll leave to your children than the inheritance you'll receive from your parents.

- Teach children in some way throughout your life.

- Too many advantages for your children add up to disadvantage.

- Take your children to lunch on a regular basis.

- Accept your children for who they are, not who you want them to be.

- The parents' role is not to make all the right choices for their children, but to teach them how to make those choices for themselves.

- Continue to be an example to your children even when they're not around.

- Teach your children to see God in the small stuff of life.

- Someday you will be a friend to your children, but you'll never stop being a parent.

- Continue to give your children room to grow throughout their lives.

- Honor your children's grandparents.

There are secret things that
belong to the Lord our God,
but the revealed things
belong to us and
our descendants forever,
so that we may obey
these words of the law.

Deuteronomy 29:29 NLT

THIRTY-SEVEN

Families Are Forever

The family must be pretty important, because Satan has been trying to destroy it since the beginning of time. We don't mean to get overly dramatic here, but we do want to take you on a little journey through history (we're going to use the Bible) and show you why this is true.

At the beginning of the Bible (and the beginning of time), God created the family. He made a man—Adam—and a woman—Eve—and put them together as a family. Then came the serpent—otherwise known as Satan—to destroy the first family by enticing them to disobey God, which they did. Only Satan didn't tear apart what God had put together. God preserved the family, and He promised that some time in the future a Savior would come from Adam and Eve's offspring (His name was Jesus) to defeat Satan.

Fast-forward to Egypt about thirty-five hundred years ago. The great Pharaoh was building his empire and his monuments on the backs of Hebrew slaves. God heard their cries and called a savior (his name was Moses) to rescue His people. Pharaoh, no doubt inspired by Satan, decided that there were too many Hebrew families. So to thin the ranks he decreed that all male babies be killed. The plan almost succeeded, except that God preserved baby Moses, who grew up to lead God's people out of Egypt. Because the Hebrew nation was spared, the family line from Adam and Eve to the future Savior was unbroken.

Fast-forward again to Palestine about two thousand years ago. King Herod, who ruled the region for Rome, heard about a new king who had been born in Bethlehem (His name was Jesus). Fearing for his throne, and no doubt inspired by Satan, Herod decreed that all Hebrew male babies be killed. Once again, God preserved the family and our future by sending an angel to Mary and Joseph, who fled to Egypt with their divine Son.

God has always had a plan to save humankind. And His plan has always involved the family. Without the family and God's efforts to preserve it, Moses and Jesus would never have been born. There would never have been a Savior for Israel and a Savior for the world.

Dr. James Dobson once said that the family is the most effective way for the Good News message to go from one generation to the next. That's why Satan wants to destroy the family: He wants to destroy the message. For that very reason, the family continues to be under attack today. Take a look at your own family. What kind of shape is it in? What are you doing to preserve and strengthen your family so your children and your children's children will be sure to hear the Good News message?

God loves your family. He knows and loves every detail about your family, and He's counting on you to help preserve it for His glory.

...In the Small Stuff

- Establish family traditions and faithfully keep them.

- Be as considerate with your family as you are with your friends.

- Be as courteous to your family as you are to strangers.

- Friendships can fade. Families are forever.

- Prefer the love of your family over the praise of acquaintances.

- There are a few nuts (and squirrels) in every family tree.

- Stay in touch with family members. It's easy to ignore those closest to you.

- Call your mother—you know how she worries.

- Send cards and notes to your grandparents on special occasions, and be sure to include current pictures of the family.

- Eat at least one meal a day together as a family.

- Develop a recreational activity your family can do together, and then enjoy it regularly.

A friend is always loyal,
and a brother is born
to help in time of need.

Proverbs 17:17 NLT

THIRTY-EIGHT

You Need Your Friends

It's easier to make friends than it is to be a friend. *Making* friends simply involves being nice to people you like. *Being* a friend, on the other hand, involves serious effort. Rather than waiting for others to make you feel better, you make it your goal to add value to their lives. That's why you can't really be a friend to very many people. It's possible to casually and superficially relate to a bunch of acquaintances at one time (kind of like working a room), but being a true friend takes time.

Being a friend is a choice. Here are four different types of friendships you could choose to be involved with. Choosing to establish these friendships will give you great fulfillment, and you will enrich the lives of others.

Be a *disciple*. A disciple is a *learner*. Find someone wiser and more spiritually mature than you are (hint: that person is probably older) so you can *learn* from him or her. Ask this person, also known as a mentor, to meet with you on a regular basis. You may want to do a Bible study together, or you may just want to talk about life.

Be a *mentor*. Even while you are being discipled, be available to teach someone else. Here's where you'll need to be patient, because a mentor doesn't usually seek out disciples. However, if you've got something to offer others and you have the time to be a friend, people will seek you out.

Be *accountable*. In this world of shifting values and vivid temptations, you need to be in an accountability group (this is especially true for men). As a group, discipline yourself to meet on a regular basis (at least once a month) to ask each other the tough questions and to discuss the tough issues.

Be a *neighbor*. When Jesus was asked to name the greatest commandment, without hesitation He replied, "Love the Lord your God," and then quickly added a second commandment: "Love your neighbor as yourself" (Mark 12:30–31 NLT). Loving your neighbor is more than lending tools or cups of sugar. It's care and concern for little things. It's sharing meaningful details from your own life. It's being a friend in such a way that your neighbor will see God in your life.

Friendships are like investments—you get what you put into them, and they take time to mature. But the dividends they pay are eternal.

...In the Small Stuff

- A friend is one whose strengths complement your weaknesses.

- Offer yourself as a friend to another. It will refresh both of you.

- Your best friends will criticize you privately and encourage you publicly.

- It's never too late to renew an old friendship.

- Friendships are built gradually but can be destroyed quickly.

- Have lots of acquaintances and a few close friends.

- Don't establish a friendship based on mutual dislikes.

- Make friends with persons of advanced years and let them know how much their friendship means.

- Make a list of six people you could count on to carry your casket at your funeral. If you can't come up with six, develop some new friendships, or plan to be cremated.

- Remember to ask friends to pray for your needs.

- A best friend can multiply your joy and divide your sorrow.

- Be loyal to your friends.

- Hold on to friendships tightly; release possessions easily.

- Select friends based on their character, not their compliments.

Don't brag about tomorrow,
since you don't know
what the day will bring.

Proverbs 27:1 NLT

THIRTY-NINE

Carpe Diem: Seize the Day

There's nothing we would enjoy more than to sit down together—just the three of us—and talk about how God works in all of our lives every day. The stories we could tell! How God's plan for each of us is unique, drawing upon our strengths and interests, yet similar because we all live for one purpose: to get to know God better.

Of course, we'd love to read about how you're getting to know God—and yourself—better each day (just send your story to our e-mail address). As for us, well, we'd like to leave you with this simple yet powerful challenge: *Carpe Diem*. It means *seize the day*.

To quote an old but effective phrase, "Today is the first day of the rest of your life." You can't do a thing to change yesterday, and only God knows for sure what is going to happen tomorrow. So today is the only day you have.

How do you seize the day? First build upon the knowledge you have that God has worked in your life in the past. Since God "never changes or casts shifting shadows" (James 1:17) you can have confidence that He will continue to work in every detail of your life. Second, have faith that God has secured your future—no matter what happens. He has given you hope.

If you live in the context of these dynamic beliefs, then you will live in God's power today. When you know that God works through your circumstances, they will energize you.

So go out and make a difference in your world. Leave an impression on everything and everyone you touch because of what God has done for you.

...In the Small Stuff

- Live life on purpose, not by accident.

- When you have the choice between taking an escalator or the stairs, take the stairs.

- Place fresh flowers in the places where you live and work.

- Visit the Holy Land once in your life.

- Once in your life, leave home on a vacation without any idea what you are going to do or where you are going to go.

- Smile at babies.

- When you develop your film, get double prints. Give the duplicates away.

- Pay attention to the design of the things you buy, and then buy the things with the best design.

- Great art brings the head and the heart together.

- Remember, there is a time for love and a place for love. Any time, any place.

- Always go the extra mile...whether for a friend or mint chocolate chip ice cream.

- An active mind is like Denny's: always open.

- Whenever you look back on your life, be positive.

- If you seek wisdom over opportunity, opportunity will usually follow.

- Change is a process, not an event.

- Follow the promptings of your heart rather than the desires of your flesh.

- Plan to be spontaneous.

- Have someone over on the spur of the moment.

- When it comes to eternity, seats are available in the smoking and the nonsmoking sections. What is your pleasure?

- Whenever you look ahead, be optimistic.

- Enjoy each day as if it were your last.

- When you spend time with God, His Word, and other people, you are investing in eternity.

- People who ask "Why?" keep others from getting things done. Those who ask "Why not?" get things done.

> "For I know the plans
> I have for you," says the Lord.
> "They are plans for good and not for disaster,
> to give you a future and a hope.
> In those days when you pray, I will listen.
> If you look for me in earnest,
> you will find me when you seek me.
> I will be found by you," says the Lord.
>
> *Jeremiah 29:11–14 NLT*

FORTY

God Is in the Small Stuff

We easily find God in nature: the majesty of a rainbow after the thunderstorm; the incredible intricacy of a colony of ants; the still, quiet of a moonlit night; or the deafening roar of the mighty Niagara Falls. God is there, and we marvel at His handiwork.

We quickly identify God's involvement in the big celebrations of our lives: the birth of a child; the new job that remedies a financial crisis; or the car crash that left the vehicle totaled but our children unscathed. God is there, and we thank Him for His provision.

And we even acknowledge God's presence in the midst of tragedy: the report from the pathology lab; the severance notice; or the heartache in a home filled with broken relationships. God is there, and we depend upon Him for strength.

But seeing God in these "big things" of life is easy. The more difficult task—yet a challenge just as rewarding—is seeing God in our everyday, mundane activities. We need to have a "God consciousness" about our daily routine. We need a "divine perspective" about the details of life. We mustn't overlook God in the small stuff.

When we realize that God is in the ordinary, our daily grind suddenly has meaning and purpose. The household chores, whether the lawn or the laundry, become an opportunity to express love and care for the other members of the household. A walk to the mailbox brings a chance to greet the neighbor (who may be in desperate need of an encouraging word). The day at work presents the challenge of giving wholehearted effort which will be pleasing to God.

Before He created the universe ages ago, God knew all about us. We should not be surprised that He has ordered our days and is interactively involved in the events of our daily routine. Nothing escapes His notice. Nothing is too insignificant for His care. If we are involved with anything, so is He.

Live your life with an overwhelming sense that God is present in the details all around you. There will be no boring moments. Life will take on new meaning when you begin to see God in the small stuff.

...In the Small Stuff

- Daily thank the Lord for His gifts.

- Display what you believe by how you behave.

- What happens in you is more important than what happens to you.

- What you think determines what you do.

- Make it a goal to always make good on your promises, no matter how long it takes.

- Learn to distinguish between opportunity and temptation.

- Anything within the scope of your responsibility will decay without your attention.

- Significance is found in the quality of work accomplished, not in the quantity of work attempted.

- As you go through the day, look for opportunities too good to miss.

- Be teachable every day.

- Have a sharp mind, a keen wit, and a discriminating tongue.

- Enjoy life's detours.

- Discover your spiritual gifts. Then, get involved in a ministry so you can use them.

- Refuse to be lazy. Take control of your time.

- Be a person of principle, passion, and purity.

- When you see God in the small stuff, your life becomes more meaningful.

About Bruce & Stan

Bruce Bickel is an attorney, but he hopes he doesn't have stay that way. Bruce and his wife, Cheryl, live in the Seattle area.

Stan Jantz was involved in Christian retail for twenty-five years before venturing into marketing and publishing. Stan and his wife, Karin, live in Ventura County, California.

Bruce & Stan have cowritten more than fifty books, including the international bestseller God Is in the Small Stuff. Their passion is to present truth in a correct, clear, and casual manner that encourages people to connect in a meaningful way with the living God.

Be sure to check out their Web site:
www.Christianity101online.com

Other Books by Bruce & Stan

God Is in the Small Stuff for Your Family
God Is in the Small Stuff for Your Marriage
God Is in the Small Stuff for Tough Times
Knowing God 101
Knowing the Bible 101
Bible Prophecy 101
Creation & Evolution 101
Growing as a Christian 101
Evidence for Faith 101
I'm Fine With God. . .It's Christians I Can't Stand
I Can't See God. . .Because I'm in the Way

ConversantLife.com

Bruce & Stan are cofounders of ConversantLife.com, a content and social media online experience designed to promote conversations about faith and culture. They encourage you to check out this site for stimulating blogs, videos, podcasts, and news.

If you have questions or comments, you can connect with Bruce & Stan at
      info@Christianity101online.com